The Class of '86

First published in Great Britain in 2006 by Linthorpe Publishing, Middlesbrough.

ISBN 978-0-9553363-2-4

Designed and printed by KallKwik, Middlesbrough.

Photo Credits
Brian Spencer, Highland Studios, Middlesbrough Evening Gazette and Martyn Harrison, Blades Sports Photography.
Additional photos taken by Alastair Brownlee and Gordon Cox.

Thanks to:
Proofreaders, Mike McGeary, Graham Bell, Eric Paylor and Sarah Donald.

The Class of '86

The rebirth of a football club

By Alastair Brownlee and Gordon Cox

Acknowledgements

Twenty years seem to have passed so quickly and yet, as a Boro fan, I can still remember the fear of possibly losing the football club I supported, followed by the joy of being able to commentate for radio on the terrific promotion season that followed the turmoil of the summer of 1986.

My first acknowledgement has to be therefore to the members of the consortium who saved the club and to the players and management who then went on to produce a style of football that restored the pride in the Boro. Producing, with Gordon, this book has been a true labour of love and I would like to thank all the players, together with Bruce Rioch and Colin Todd, who gave their time so freely and so openly.

The choice of which players to include was a difficult one, but in the end Gordon and I decided that we would concentrate on the twelve players who took part in the opening game against Port Vale plus Gary Pallister who was suspended. I'm sorry if that has excluded players who made a contribution that season, but their efforts have not been forgotten and are referred to in the comprehensive statistics section at the end of this book.

Jonathan Woodgate kindly agreed to write the foreword as his tribute to a team that gave him the inspiration to become a professional footballer.

I would like to thank Graham Fordy for providing a valuable insight into the consortium and the financial battle to save the club.

Dave Allan has, as always, been a great help and his book written with Adrian Bevington, *Doom to Boom*, was an invaluable read and I would strongly recommend it to all Boro fans who want to know not only about 1986, but the decade that followed.

Tracking down the players has been, thankfully, a relatively easy task, but Diane O'Connell was a great help in putting me in touch with Gary Hamilton who now lives in Texas, USA.

Bernie Slaven was not only a key member of the squad but has spent time on many away trips with me, for Century fm, in encouraging this book be finished as a tribute to a great team. He also filled in some of the gaps when my memory failed. Thank you Bernard!

Thanks are also due to all the proofreaders for giving their time to help produce the finished article.

As always, family tends to suffer when a book is being researched and written, so my wife Wendy, together with daughters Alison and Emily, have put up with me as the centre of my world for a few weeks focused on 1986 and not their needs in 2006. Sorry.

My mam and dad, Mavis and Malcolm, are great supporters throughout all the projects I get involved with, so thanks again.

Finally, I hope that you, the reader, enjoy the book. The aim was to enable you to go back to a time when a group of players, largely homegrown, under the guidance of a manager who believed in playing attractive football, thought they could take on the world in the name of Middlesbrough Football Club and win. They remain to this day my heroes.

Alastair Brownlee

If you learn from those who make a positive difference and have the ability to share what you learn with others then you will achieve much in life.

Treat people with the respect they deserve, live life properly and with dignity. Always have a dream, always have belief and never give up.

Philosophies epitomised by Bruce Rioch and Tony Mowbray 20 years ago, values which still hold strong today. Thanks to them for what they helped achieve, to Steve Gibson for his driving ambition which gave the consortium direction and to the players of that time, each and every one, for making sure the legacy of a football club in Middlesbrough not only continued, but flourished.

Gordon Cox

Contents

Quotation

"You know we just don't recognise
the most significant moments of our lives
while they're happening.
Back then I thought, well, there'll be other days.
I didn't realise that that was the only day."

Dr. Archibald "Moonlight" Graham in the 1989 film *Field of Dreams*.

Foreword

It is a fantasy what has been achieved with Middlesbrough Football Club since they were in Division Three 20 years ago.

Cup finals, Europe and the Premiership, it's magnificent. If someone had said back in 1986 that we would achieve all that in the next 20 years, you would think they were completely mad.

I used to love going to the games. My grandad used to live in the Brompton Street area. I used to go there and just walk down to Ayresome Park, get a squeeze in and sit on my dad's knee, there were all good times.

I was too young to fully understand what was going on that summer. But I remember there was a programme on the telly about it and Chris Rea was in the background doing the Steel River song. I remember the gates being locked and everyone just hoping that the club survived.

Gary Pallister was my idol and Tony Mowbray a legend as captain, but I could name the team from one to eleven, starting with Stephen Pears, now there was a proper goalkeeper, he was the best in the world wasn't he?

What would Middlesbrough, as a town, have done without the football team? Everyone is very lucky to have this club and it's fantastic what it's gone on to achieve.

It's what dreams are made of. Mr Gibson had a plan and he has fulfilled that, well in part, I think there is much more to come. He's still ambitious in every way.

Jonathan Woodgate.
England, Real Madrid and the Boro.

Introduction

On Wednesday May 10 2006, Middlesbrough Football Club were led out by captain Gareth Southgate to compete in the final of the UEFA Cup. On that balmy evening in Eindhoven it seemed unthinkable that just 20 years previously the club were fighting for their very existence following relegation to Division Three.

Financial problems which had been building for many years finally came to a head in the summer of 1986 and a consortium battled to save professional football in Middlesbrough. Their efforts only succeeded with 37 minutes left before a Football League deadline.

Had the consortium failed, the implications were stark. Boro's fixture list for the 1986-87 season would have been null and void. The amazing journey that would go on to include promotions, Wembley cup finals, Carling Cup glory, world class names pulling on the red shirt and the Riverside Stadium would have ended before it began in a London hotel on August 22 1986.

In truth, long before the summer of 1986, Boro had been on a downward spiral. The Jack Charlton years of the mid-seventies, when Ayresome Park was packed with crowds of over 30,000 watching top flight football, were a distant memory and disillusioned supporters deserted the club in ever-growing numbers, to such an extent that when the club was relegated to Division Three gates hovered around the 6,000 mark.

The key moment for many Boro fans was when young stars started leaving the club after John Neal's side lost an FA Cup quarter-final replay at Wolves on March 10 1981. Their quality wasn't replaced and suspicion grew about the way the club was being run from the boardroom. As Steve Gibson recalled in *Doom To Boom*, "Charles Amer was the chairman of Middlesbrough Football Club and Parkway Estates did internal work for the club, including the building of a controversial sports complex. I have actually seen a letter that was written by Graham Kelly, then secretary of the Football League, to Charles Amer, asking how he was to finance the sports complex because he was applying for grant aid. Amer replied it would be with the sale of players, Armstrong, Proctor, Johnston and Hodgson. That letter is still in the possession of Middlesbrough Football Club."

By 1986 the club needed a vast input of cash to survive and the plan, led by Gibson, was to pull together a consortium to save it. Gibson, as a fan, realised how important the club was to an area which was suffering high rates of unemployment that reached 28 per cent in some parts. Clearly the last thing needed was for the supporters to lose their club.

Although the debt was crippling at the time, in modern terms it wasn't that large, as Graham Fordy, now Commercial Manager and back in 1986 a consortium member, reflects. "In total it was about £2.9m, which is nothing compared to the current situation in football, where some players earn more than that in a season. But back then it was seen as a catastrophic debt for a football club.

"John Foster, Middlesbrough Borough Council's chief executive, was a great help in using his connections and the council approached ICI, a major employer in the town, while Steve Gibson approached Scottish and Newcastle Breweries where I worked. In addition, an advert was placed in *The Times* for interested parties to come forward. This prompted businessman Henry Moszkowicz to join."

Momentum was building. Colin Henderson became ICI's representative and his involvement was to become critical, as the deadline imposed by the Football League grew perilously close.

John Foster allowed council offices to be used for meetings and it was from the town hall that the players would receive their wages, once the consortium had opened the necessary bank accounts and started to accumulate funds. Negotiations with creditors were key, as Fordy recalls. "We contacted everyone who was owed money by the old club and offered them terms for settlement of about 50p in the pound to try to reach agreement. The only exception was Charles Amer, whose actions when he was chairman we believed had led the club into this position and we felt he should not be paid a penny."

Gibson was a board member of the football club and had taken total executive powers after a heated board meeting. From this position he was able to wind up the old football club, so that the consortium could take Middlesbrough FC forward without the existing shareholders benefiting from their hard work. This action required the agreement of the Football League, and the concern was that after several clubs had used the liquidation route to survive, leaving huge unpaid debts, the League might make an example of Middlesbrough. This fear was to turn into reality.

Meanwhile, the consortium battled on and with the support of its backers had the capability of raising £900,000, which they believed was enough to pay the creditors the agreed reduced terms. But all their efforts looked to have been in vain when disastrously the council withdrew their £200,000 stake. Fordy remembers the moment. "I was disappointed with their actions. I believe we were caught in a battle of political parties. I remember after the club was saved I went to a friend's party, where a councillor in my hearing said it would have been better for the club to die once and for all with all the problems it caused the Ayresome ward! I left the party early. It summed up for me the political problems we had faced in some quarters. I think John Foster was a great help to us, but the council let us down."

The gap in finances was partly bridged by Moszkowicz putting in another £150,000 and Gibson finding £25,000. The consortium believed they had enough funds, but on the Thursday before the opening game, ICI's solicitors had news - and it wasn't good. "They said the Football League were happy to proceed with the settlement of creditors. But in addition to the funds we had raised, a bond for £1.9m had to be lodged with their bank. This would guarantee that if creditors had to be paid in full, pound for pound, they could be. It was a terrible night and seemed an impossible task, like going to bed with your only hope being your lottery numbers all coming up! But during the night Colin Henderson, who was back on Teesside because of illness to his mother, spoke to Sir John Harvey Jones at the highest level of ICI and somehow got agreement that the chemical giant ICI would deliver the bond. To this day I am not sure how he was able to do it. But by achieving it he had saved the club."

There was still work to do on the Friday as consortium members sat in one room in a London hotel and Football League representatives sat in another, passing notes backwards and forwards. However the confirmation of the bond at 11am meant the consortium had what they needed to fulfill the Football League criteria. In the end the document wasn't signed until minutes before the deadline. But the Boro had been saved.

Colin Henderson was to be the chairman of Middlesbrough Football & Athletic Company (1986) Limited, with Gibson, Fordy, Reg Corbidge and Moszkowicz on the board. Despite differing financial contributions, each board member had one vote.

At a press conference at Middlesbrough town hall, Colin Henderson and Steve Gibson announced that the club had been saved and would play the next day at Hartlepool's ground against Port Vale.

The spotlight now switched to the players and management of Middlesbrough Football Club. Their story is the main theme of this book but without the hard work of the consortium their career paths would have been very different. "The team of '86 wasn't really important until we kicked off at Hartlepool. Until then, the prime motive was the financial survival of the club," says Fordy. "We left it up to Bruce Rioch to make sure that a squad would be ready. Once the team started to play they had a run of great success for three seasons and the turmoil of the summer, I am sure, bonded them together. As the games progressed I got very close to them and I am very proud that the friendships established then are still strong today."

The third division campaign kicked off on August 23 1986. What followed, forged out of the stress and strain of the summer, was a remarkable achievement. How the club went from liquidation to promotion is one of football's true fairytales. And it's time for the players and management to take centre stage. This is their story.

1. Bruce Rioch

Manager, Middlesbrough Football Club February 1986 to March 1990

Born: Aldershot September 6 1947

Current Occupation: Manager, Odense Football Club, Denmark.

As the son of a Regimental Sergeant Major, keeping discipline came naturally to Bruce Rioch.

Early in 2006 I travelled to Denmark to meet up with him to reflect on the dramatic events twenty years earlier in which, as manager, he had played a pivotal role.

On the journey, I reflected upon my relationship with Bruce in '86 when, as a young commentator on BBC Radio Cleveland, I must admit to having been in awe of the manager. He was such an imposing figure that you rehearsed your questions well in advance of any interview, just to make sure you didn't get on the wrong side of a man who clearly had an iron grip on the dressing room.

As a fan, however, I loved the Rioch style of football that brought the club back to life and the supporters back on to the terraces. Quite simply, he put the football heart back into a decaying club and for that, fans of that time still refer to him fondly as 'Sir Bruce'.

The Rioch I met in Denmark, like all of us, is older and has mellowed. Sometimes you feel he is a little embarrassed when talk turns to the way he made such an indelible mark on his squad (as a young coach). But his love of football still beats as strongly as ever, and so does his pride for his boys, the class of '86.

Casting his mind back two decades, Bruce recalled that the storm clouds of the liquidation crisis came early in the summer. "I remember Steve Gibson and other board members assembling all the staff in the boardroom at Ayresome Park and delivering the immortal words, 'I am here to inform you that the football club is going into provisional liquidation.' Immediately we all wondered what would happen with jobs and positions and I looked at Ken Smith and Joe Hunt, the kit managers, together with Sally, the tea lady, all people who had been associated with the club for years, now unemployed."

The manager had made his decision to stick with the club, living in digs in the Acklam area of Middlesbrough while keeping his family home in Birmingham and never losing his faith that the club would survive. "I went on a family holiday to Majorca and two days into my break, I received a phone call from the temporary chief executive acting for the provisional liquidator. He said, 'Unfortunately I have to inform you that your contract at Middlesbrough Football Club has been terminated. You have two options, one is to leave the club and the second is to continue to work but without salary.' It was a difficult moment, as I had a wife and children, but I decided to work on.'

The consortium had been set up to try to solve the financial issues and Bruce asked for an assurance from them. "All I said was that if we were to go under, then they must let me know directly rather than me hearing it on radio, or reading it in a newspaper, so I could inform the players. Once I had that agreement, I gathered the players and gave them my assurance. 'Until you hear from me personally that this club is going out of existence, we will continue to focus and prepare for the new season,' I told them I felt it was important that I gave a largely young group of young footballers some stability."

Drawing on his military background, it's hard not to see Bruce invoking a Dunkirk spirit among the staff as the summer unfolded. "On one occasion, the water board came to turn off the water at Ayresome Park as the bill hadn't been paid. I found out the supply was also due to be turned off at the training ground, Hutton Road. I asked the workers to go and switch off Hutton Road first so I could fill a bath with water at Ayresome. After they left I drove my car over the manhole cover so they couldn't turn off the water when they came back, I then went to the town to find a member of the consortium to give me £300-£400 to pay the bill to keep the water on for the players' showers!"

Finding cash was a theme. "Our coach driver, Mervyn, came to me as we were due to play a reserve game at Coventry. He was refusing to drive the team there, as the football club hadn't paid his bills. I persuaded him to take the team otherwise we would be fined. Again I went into town, somehow found £1,000, drove to Coventry and gave Mervyn the money so he could keep his business going and also keep the coach available to us."

The manager's pockets had to run deep. "I paid all the YTS wages, all the lodgings for the YTS lads and other players in digs, together with the maintenance and service payments for kit men Ken Smith and Joe Hunt. I also paid for my own lodge with Mrs Crombie on Acklam Road. This was at a time when I wasn't getting paid myself!"

For some players, naturally, thoughts turned to possibly moving on. "It was tough for them. They had to queue at the town hall for wages. Earlier in the summer I had released 20 players, leaving me just 15 to work with. Of that group I really wanted to keep Peter Beagrie, but the club couldn't offer him a contract so he went to Sheffield United. I knew that Gary Pallister had gone to Crystal Palace for talks (until years later) he didn't know I was aware of it! A friend of mine had spotted him with Ron Noades, then Crystal Palace chairman, who was on the panel of the League deciding the Boro's future..."

Thankfully the consortium saved the club and thoughts turned to the first game of the season against Port Vale. "I had been in Steve Gibson's office earlier that week when the chief of police rang to say they needed to know within one hour if the game was going ahead, otherwise we couldn't use Ayresome Park. I passed on the message to the consortium, but they were still finalising everything and so we eventually got permission to use the Victoria Ground, Hartlepool. Getting ready for the game we borrowed their physio Tommy Johnson, who later joined us, and Tony Mowbray asked Tommy for a massage before the game. Tommy replied; 'Hartlepool have the cheapest bill for rubbing oil in the Football League - we don't have any!' So Tony never got his massage."

Tony Mowbray was Bruce Rioch's rock. "Tony was a great captain and a very special person. After games at Ayresome he would leave the players' lounge and take Ken Smith home in his car before coming back to rejoin his family. That tells you what a caring person he was. He was a great human being and the greatest captain I was involved with throughout my career."

Pride began to come back to the club. "I gathered all the players and staff together and asked them to paint the stadium, as it looked shabby and dilapidated. They agreed and we painted all the crash barriers red and generally smartened up what was our home and place of work. The crowds started to come back as they could see the entertainment we were providing on the pitch and the next two or three years were phenomenal."

There was only one moment when Bruce thought about leaving and ironically it came after the club had solved their financial problems and were on the up. "The board met and the chairman, Colin Henderson, offered me a three-month contract. I said no. After all I had been through, the liquidation period and keeping the players together when I had no salary. I was not accepting a three-month deal and drove back to Birmingham. To be fair, Colin Henderson then rang and offered a three-year deal. They had reconsidered and I agreed. I can understand in a way that some of the consortium didn't know me and they were still sorting finances out, but I wasn't going to stay for a three-month deal and thankfully it didn't come to that."

The club were on the upward spiral after years of relegation fears. "I used to set targets. 'Let's keep twenty clean sheets. If you achieve that and with our ability to score with Archie and Bernie, then we will win football matches.' In the run-in to the end of the season, we only conceded one goal in the last seven games, winning six. Promotion brought great scenes of joy and everyone had contributed to our success."

In recent times, Middlesbrough have won silverware and reached a UEFA Cup final, but 1986 remains a key moment in the club's history. Says Rioch: "Nothing would have been possible without '86 and the work of Steve Gibson, Colin Henderson and the rest of the consortium to find the money to save the club. Then there were the staff and players. In reality, there are a group of 20 to 30 people who Middlesbrough Football Club can thank for saving them and then making all the success of today possible."

Bruce remains proud of his players. "I spoke to someone three months ago who said, 'Do you realise that the players from '86 who you worked with at Boro all had fine careers and were never involved in any problems off the pitch?' That says a lot about the boys, good backgrounds, good families. The group I had there were mainly young men making their way in the football world. They were young enough to be my sons. I realise that some of the standards I set might have been severe, but that group of players from 1986 to 1988 carried themselves through their careers impeccably on and off the pitch, and that's a great credit to them."

And also to you, Bruce.

2. Colin Todd

First team coach and Bruce Rioch's assistant from 1986 to 1990

Born: Chester-le-Street December 12 1948

Current Occupation: Manager of Bradford City FC

Colin Todd was working for Vaux Breweries when he was reunited with a former Derby County team mate during a game at Hartlepool.

Bruce Rioch had taken over from Willie Maddren as manager of Middlesbrough in February 1986, while Todd had fancied a change of scenery after an illustrious playing career, which included a highly-successful stay at the Baseball Ground alongside the man he was now sitting next to at the Victoria Ground.

It was a chance meeting which was to lead to the duo guiding Boro from the brink of despair to two successive promotions, before relegation and a parting of the ways.

Todd takes up the story. "Not long after meeting with Bruce I got a phone call from him. He'd just taken over from Willie and asked if I was interested in working with him at Ayresome Park. I'd been out of the game a year. I didn't think I would miss it, but I did, terribly, so I said yes, I'd love to. But soon there was only him, chief scout Barry Geldart and myself of the backroom staff left. The rest had gone and within a week of me giving up my job with the brewery, the club went into administration.

"We weren't getting paid until a consortium put some money into an account which allowed us to take the players to the town hall every week, identify them, and enable them to get some money.

"The gates at Ayresome were closed and we called ourselves the gypsies because we used to travel to different venues for training. But out of that adversity, we didn't half become strong."

The success which followed that season was in no small measure down to the players, says Todd. "They really gelled. In part that was because of the adversity of that summer, but they were good players with ability. We got the best out of them, but they matured very quickly and they became men.

"It just shows you that if you have a group of players who want it badly enough, you can succeed. In the time that Bruce, myself and Barry were together we restored pride and status back to the club.

"The pedigree Bruce and I had as players helped – I think you'll see that with Roy Keane at Sunderland - that and the fact the team were largely made up of local boys. It was a mix which worked. The players had confidence in us and we had confidence in them. There was a lot of hard work put in, but not once did they shirk it and we all got our rewards in the end."

While Rioch was always seen as the disciplinarian, Todd was perceived as the shoulder to cry on.

"You change when you become a manager," he admits. "You have to not quite distance yourself, but keep yourself not so close to them. Bruce was the one who would give the rollickings, if you like, I had to pick them up ready for the second half.

"It's fair to say I learned a lot from Bruce's management, but we were a good team. It worked exactly the same for us when we worked together at Bolton later on.

"When Bruce has worked on his own, it's not quite gelled for him. We haven't always seen eye to eye and we had our disagreements, especially later on. There were mistakes made, but we were always man enough to admit them and put them right.

"We were two strong voices and when I got my feet under the table we would sit and talk about players, examine and discuss the opposition, assess teams. We'd have different opinions, but it didn't affect our relationship. Sometimes Bruce could be stubborn, very stubborn, and it made it difficult at times, as people would tell you. But we worked together to get the best out of the players."

Part of the art of man-management is working with a group of people of varying strength of character. This was something Todd and Rioch did particularly well.

"Archie Stephens was a strong character in his own right and Bernie Slaven was a stubborn old bugger. Bernie was Bernie, he had to be the one. He was the one who would have tantrums and spit his dummy out. I remember one game I took him off at half-time and he was home by the start of the second half!

"Even though Gary Pallister had come from non-league he was a leader out there, Tony Mowbray was a leader and Gary Hamilton was the inspiration in the dressing room. Stephen Pears and Gary Parkinson were quiet and frightened of the manager, while Colin Cooper was quite strong, but the team became stronger and stronger by winning games. They knitted together.

"The one thing which could have destroyed us was injuries, but we didn't have any - well only one, Brian Laws. The players played through knocks, but they were treated well. Sometimes they didn't train during the week, we just got them ready to play the next game. Physio Tommy Johnson used to take them to Redcar and into the sea. I think that was enough!"

As we sat in the main stand at Bradford City's Valley Parade, we enjoyed an elevated position over a landscape which has changed dramatically over the years. Parallels can be drawn with Middlesbrough. Both towns are products of the Industrial Revolution in the 1800s, but while Teesside was steel, so Bradford led the way with textiles, particularly wool. These days, as with the steel mills, the woollen mills are largely quiet.

Todd, though, draws another parallel. "When I took over here we were in administration, people worked tirelessly to help the club survive and we've been okay for around three years now. I honestly believe that the passion of the fans in the north-east wouldn't have allowed Boro to fold. If we had finished fifth off bottom and stayed in the Third Division, then there would still have been a football club. In my mind there always would be.

"I think everyone at that time helped stabilise the football club. Bryan Robson took it on to the next level and it's snowballed. Steve Gibson learned from the difficult times 20 years ago and the club is unrecognisable from then."

Todd was to take over from Rioch as manager shortly before Boro's first appearance in a Wembley final, the Zenith Data Systems against Chelsea in 1990, when the side was led out by Tony Mowbray.

"That was my gesture to Tony," Todd admits. "I could have led them out - Bruce would have done - but Tony was injured and couldn't play. As a manager you have to make decisions and I thought it was the right thing to do.

"The keys to being a successful manager are man management and the signing of players. We never really had the opportunity to strengthen at Middlesbrough because of circumstances, but you learn from the good people. I worked with Cloughie, Jim Smith, Sir Alf Ramsey and I learned a lot. What happened in the early days with Middlesbrough stood me in great stead for the future."

It was a future which was to see him manage at Bolton, Swindon and Derby, before taking the reins at Bradford City. Colin had stayed overnight with his son Andy in Bolton the night before we met. Major traffic problems on the M62 had meant the 40-mile journey had taken four-and-a-half hours and he was not in a happy mood when he arrived. But by the time we'd finished our chat, the memories of his time with Boro had calmed the frustration and brought a smile to his face.

"I've had some good days in football, really good days, but I look back on my time with Middlesbrough in 1986 as great days. I look at the game now and there are foreigners all over, some good, some not. But they were by and large local boys which pulled the club together and helped everyone back then.

"We've all drifted apart to a degree, but the memories are always there. From the moment we learned that there may not be a club anymore, we all pulled in the same direction. That was the key. Everyone wanted to take the club further."

On the way home I drove through the edge of a tornado. Rain slammed horizontally into the car and debris flew around at roof height – perhaps the meteorological equivalent of what was going on behind the scenes in 1986. This day, like then, there was sunshine just around the corner.

Thanks Colin, not just for your time and your thoughts, but for what you did for the club 20 years ago.

3. Tony Mowbray: Number 4

Born: Saltburn November 22 1963

From: Juniors in 1981

Season 1986-87: 58 appearances. Seven goals

Current Occupation: Manager of Hibernian FC in the Scottish Premier League

Edinburgh is a beautiful city and Scotland's capital was bathed in warm, late-summer sun as I met up with the captain of the Class of '86 in the seats in the main stand at Easter Road.

Mowbray earned respect, set high standards and was as durable as the ore once mined from the hills which rise a little to the north-west of his Saltburn birthplace. Tony Mowbray led by example.

A little older than most of his team mates in the summer of '86, Mogga was Bruce Rioch's idea of a captain and handed him the armband – he was perceived by several of his team mates as, 'The chosen one', Bruce's favourite.

Tony took it all with the dignity and strength of character which were to become trademarks throughout his career.

"I may have been captain, but I didn't know much more than the rest of the lads that summer," he reveals. "There was a lot of uncertainty, a lot of waiting around radios waiting for news, waiting to see what was going to happen.

"A lot of credit must go to Bruce and Toddy for keeping things going. Here I am on the other side of the fence now, manager of Hibernian, organising training sessions with the players, making sure they know what they're doing and where they've got to be because we don't have a training ground. We beg steal and borrow from the local council. We're in Edinburgh, where land is massively expensive, but I have been pushing my chairman for around two years now and we have just bought a farm on the outskirts of the city by-pass and we are to turn it into a training ground.

"It was very much like that in '86. I remember training at Billingham Synthonia where we threw jumpers down for goalposts, using scraggy balls, not new balls like clubs get at the start of a season. Bruce and Toddy used to try and make the sessions as enjoyable as possible and together they were a good combination.

"They were so competitive and were probably still better players than any of us. You didn't want to get on the wrong side of them in training or you'd get kicked, they were that competitive. With Bruce standards were so high and I aspire to them to this day.

"Some of the players struggled with the standards set and maybe they don't talk too well of him, although I'm sure they respect him for what he did to their careers. I was okay with it. He was pretty strict, looking back he probably had to be. The only way he could stop us from being anything other than a rabble, training on school fields with no goalposts, was to keep us disciplined and well-organised and make us feel professional, even if the resources we had at the club didn't suggest we were.

"We could have been a non-league club training on a Thursday night. We could have been sucked into the scenario of, 'We don't have anything, what right have we to win football matches?'. But out of that adversity comes a steeliness, it certainly did with those players.

"I'd like to think I had been brought up with it. My father was a steelworker all his life and instilled a grittiness into you. Gary Hamilton came from a tough background in Glasgow and that fight is within certain individuals, it's inbred. I didn't have a tough upbringing, my influences in my life were from my father basically. He was a working class guy who had worked all his life in the steel industry doing scaffolding. It was bred into you to stand your corner and work hard and fight for what you believed in."

There are numerous examples of how Mowbray and his team displayed those noble characteristics throughout the season. They were called for from an early stage.

"I remember the second game of the season at Wigan," says the skipper. "It was the first time I had seen Bruce use outside material to motivate his team. You can talk all you want as a football manager, but there has to be something else."

The walls around the dressing room at Hibernian's Easter Road home are bedecked with photographs and quotations from great moments and people in history.

"A lot of that comes from Bruce," admits Mowbray. "The quotations teach you a lot, but what I try to teach my players is humility. This day at Wigan, I think Paul Jewell was playing for them, we came off at half-time time level but we'd been battered. Two of their players said, 'This lot are shit, we'll beat them easy, we just have to keep at it because they're poor'. Bruce used that as part of his team talk. He'd heard those players running us down. It worked perfectly and we went out and won 2-0. After what we had come through that summer, for some opposition player to come out with that just had the effect of giving us a launch pad. Bruce didn't like it and challenged us to go and do something about it."

Mowbray admits that details of the games that season, though, are by and large a blur. "I'm not one for memories like that, I don't hang on to things, I just live for the next day. But there are certain times which stick with you. It was a case of young players being thrust in and carrying the torch for the football club and a manager wanting us to play a style of football which was an education to us. The whole experience was an education.

"I was a young player who had aspired to be a footballer all my life. To get into the team and realise that it wasn't that enjoyable when you were struggling, changed the way you lived your life.

"It wasn't always a good thing to be a Boro player. When I was 18, 19, 20-years-old I was part of a team which people didn't want to grasp on to. The perception of the average teenage Boro fan living in Redcar that summer, and for a few before, was that we were rubbish. They would be walking down the street and you could hear them, 'Look, there's Tony Mowbray', followed by some sarcastic remark as we'd just been beaten again. It wasn't a good thing to be a footballer then and I found it hard."

That perception soon changed.

"Those same people who had been calling me and the team were now looking across and saying, 'Look, there's God over there'. They were almost bowing down. Redcar is a pretty small place and you know the circles these people move in. For those people to change their view of us all was such an enjoyable turnaround for me.

"To have been transformed from a side which had struggled and eventually been relegated, to one which restored pride in the local community was great for me.

"It's been the same at Hibs, where we've finished third and fifth, in the two years I've been here. People want to wear the shirt again, they want to be in the club shop and associated with the team once more."

But was Mowbray ever tempted to move on during the dark days? "I don't think

I was a good enough player," he says openly. "I don't think there was a lot of interest in me. Joe Royle has admitted since that he made an enquiry when he was with Oldham, but that was about it. I remember sitting with Bruce at Maiden Castle, where we used to train, and talking about a contract after a second successive promotion. These were the days before agents and I was told to go and think about what I was worth. I had no idea.

"Pally and I seemed to be the ones who were the focal point of the team's success and we were the ones offered new contracts. I remember Pally talking figures and I said, 'You can't be asking for that,' and I don't know what he got in the end. I got a pretty modest amount, but it wasn't about the money.

"I was a lad from Redcar who had supported his team since he was eight, wanted to play for it and was now captain of it."

The fanzine *Fly Me To The Moon* was named after a comment made by Rioch about his skipper who he said he would take to the moon with him. It was a phrase which brought Mowbray a fair amount of stick in the dressing room.

"I'm proud that people have named something after me from an era which is still talked about today. I know the club have gone on to great things, but there are people who love the club with a passion who still talk about the team from '86. Even though they have been to a UEFA Cup final and won a League Cup final, this is still the era they talk about. Maybe there was more pride then, or maybe just as much pride, as in anything else which has gone on since. They are still as good as any football memories you will have for the rest of your lives, really."

Mowbray eventually moved on from Middlesbrough and made his mark with Glasgow Celtic. The trademark players' huddle at the start of each game was started by him in 1994. "The experiences I had there were incredible. The fans in Glasgow are either Rangers or Celtic, nothing in the middle. If you walk to the corner store there are 15 people who want to talk about the game. If you go to the supermarket it can take you three hours to finish your shop because people want to tell you how good or bad you were the previous week. I used to drive home to Middlesbrough every Saturday night and back up on the Sunday night because I was on my own. But I met my first wife two years into my stay and we had great times until her death from breast cancer.

"The warmth from the whole Celtic community in the aftermath of that cemented a relationship with the supporters of the club that remains strong today. On the pitch, though, it wasn't the greatest time of my life. Rangers were in the middle of their nine titles in a row and we were playing at Hampden as Parkhead was being developed. The board was replaced, so were two managers, and we weren't the best of teams."

From there he moved to Ipswich. He scored a headed goal at Wembley that got his team back into a play-off final which they went on to win in his final game as a player in professional football. "That catapulted us into the Premiership and we finished fifth and played in Europe against Inter Milan the following season.

"That goal is what the fans talk about when I go back there. We built a superb training complex on the back of that promotion and the club built new stands," he says with pride. "I was a coach under George Burley there, after four good playing years."

A move back north of the border brought his first managerial position. "Maybe the legacy I leave here will be the training ground, which was a million miles away when I first joined. Then the club were making £2 to £3m losses every season, now we're making profits. The crowd has doubled, the team are functioning and people like what's happening."

There was a large part of Teesside hoping that when Steve McClaren left Middlesbrough in the summer of 2006, the Prodigal Son would return home. Was he aware of the interest?

"Only because my mother lives in Redcar and my sister in Guisborough. They read papers, read websites and listen to the Three Legends phone-in, where fans leave their opinions in one form or another.

"Middlesbrough never came, I never had any conversation with anybody from there, it never happened. I obviously didn't fit the profile of the manager Mr Gibson and Mr Lamb were looking for. They are very, very professional people who knows what they want in a manager for their football club. If they decide I'm not the guy they want to manage their team, then who am I to say anything? My life is built around humility, respect and honour. Who am I to be arrogant enough to think I would be in with a chance of managing them because I played for them 15 years ago?

"Is it a job I would love? Well, the Premier League is where all managers want to be. I want to pick a team which can outfox Sir Alex Ferguson and Jose Mourinho, even though they've got millions more than I've got to spend.

"I want to be cleverer than them, I want to put my players in positions on the pitch – like I do when we play Celtic and Rangers, who have 20 times the budget we've got – and beat teams. I remember last season we beat Rangers 3-0 at Ibrox and it's a great feeling when you can put a bunch of kids out there and give them the motivation and the formation which will hurt the opposition.

"When I go home after a match and we've lost, it's like somebody has kicked me in the stomach, stabbed you in the heart and continued to wrench it around. It's your team, you've picked it, you've made the substitutions and had all the fans there wanting you to do well. At times you feel like you've let them all down – it becomes personal.

"I like to think that I'm a nice guy, but when it comes to the passion of football and there's somebody in that dressing room who's not doing it, it's not about the player. It's about the community, it's about pulling on the jersey for the punters. I want all my players to earn big bucks, drive big cars and have big houses, but I want the fans to have a team to be proud of, and for that team to earn respect."

Mowbray says there are many parallels to be drawn between the Hibernian team of today and the Middlesbrough team of 1986, not least the look of the players.

"They have blonde spiky haircuts and a lot of peroxide," he says laughing. "They are a talented young team with no training ground, but I think the club is going places. I'm doing what I want to do, being a football manager and moulding young men into a team and enjoying it along the way.

"I remain ambitious. I would love to manage in the Premiership and be cleverer than the next man. While the league is inevitably won by the team with the most money, you can punch above your weight. Your philosophy of play is what wins football matches week in, week out and while as a manager you seem to have everybody's lives in your hands, you can still try to play football which is pleasing to the eye.

"I want to win and I want to play that way. It's about getting the balance right and I'm enjoying the journey."

If the gods are kind, Tony Mowbray's journey will be long, successful and richly rewarding. He deserves it.

4. Stephen Pears: Number 1

Born: Brandon January 22 1962

From: Manchester United £80,000

Season 1986-87: 58 appearances, 32 clean sheets

Current Occupation: Goalkeeping coach at Middlesbrough FC Academy

It's an over-used phrase, but first impressions last. Driving to Middlesbrough's Rockliffe Park training HQ, the words came instantly to mind as I thought about interviewing Stephen Pears, the great goalkeeper of the class of '86.

As a commentator for BBC Radio Cleveland, my first impression of Stephen came on November 5 1983 as he made his Boro debut, on loan from Manchester United, in front of 7,686 fans against Cardiff City at Ayresome Park. Boro under Malcolm Allison were going through a tough spell. They had lost five out of the previous six games, conceding 11 goals - not the greatest time for a keeper to make his mark. But not only did he keep a clean sheet in a 2-0 win, he also left the impression that if Cardiff had played until midnight they wouldn't have scored. He really was that good.

It was the best debut from a goalkeeper I could remember and he proved it was no fluke in a six-game spell during which he kept four clean sheets. An appeal was launched to try to raise the £60,000 Manchester United wanted for his services but despite thousands being promised the target couldn't be reached and instead United offered Pears a three-year-deal. Thankfully, Willie Maddren brought him back on a permanent basis and 23 years after his debut Pears is still part of the Boro set-up, teaching the next generation of goalkeepers.

As we enjoyed a coffee at the state-of-the-art training ground it was hard not to contrast the club in 2006 with the one he first played for in 1983. "Manchester United's set up back then was similar to Boro's today and as a player you were spoilt: kit laid out for you, great training facilities. At Boro I took my first team kit home and washed it myself. I used to buy my own goalkeeper's shirt and take it to the bloke's house where the outfield players' kit was made in Stanley, County Durham to have the Boro logo put on. I remember Colin Cooper cleaning his own boots even when he was in the first team, but that's just the way it was."

The lure of coming back to the north-east and first team football was the motivation behind the loan deal of 1983 and then the permanent move. "My first manager here was Big Mal and he was a great character to play for. He used to train me personally on the pitch, which was unusual for a manager. Later I came back for Willie Maddren. Willie said he wanted to build the team around me. Things didn't go well for him but Bruce Rioch was lucky that so many good young players were there when he took the job."

Despite being happy back in the north-east, the summer of '86 was tough. "I remember after getting relegated at Shrewsbury thinking 'what have I done?'. Coming from Manchester United I was facing football in Division Three and a bleak financial future. Living in Durham, there was no *Evening Gazette* to keep up to date with what was going on, so I was on the phone to the other lads talking about the situation and having to dig into my savings to make ends meet. But I always thought the club would survive."

Training for a specialist position like goalkeeper was also difficult. "Peter Flear was the other keeper and we were taken aside from the other players for an hour. He was only young so I had to tell him the work I needed and then I helped him, but to be honest the principles of goalkeeping don't alter. I was taught at United by Harry Gregg, who was fantastic, and I still use what he taught me when I am working with the young keepers today."

Then there was the Rioch factor. "I got on well with Bruce, I was 24 and he rarely had a go at me. He was inspirational with his team talks, the best in all my career, and he really made you want to go out and play. I have heard so many managers' talks over the years and you can get a bit blasé, but he left you feeling that you had to do well for him and the club.

"Bruce just lived for football. You could get on the coach for an away game at Plymouth and he would still be talking football when you got back to Ayresome Park. He did have his disagreements with players and with the younger ones he could rule with fear. I remember some horrendous blazers and ties that we had to wear and on one trip to the USA it was boiling hot and we asked if we could take them off. The reply? 'I don't think so gentlemen. You are representing Middlesbrough Football Club.' So we continued to sweat."

If Archie Stephens and Bernie Slaven were crucial to promotion by virtue of the goals they scored, the defence was watertight. "Thirty clean sheets tells the story. Tony Mowbray was the best centre-half I played behind in my career, Gary Pallister was a bit lazy then but look at his career. At full-back Colin Cooper, who would go on to play for England, and Gary Parkinson, who was a good player who didn't get the recognition he deserved. In a way he was similar to Gary Gill, who played a great role in front of the back four in '86, but for whatever reason Bruce didn't keep faith with him the season after and that was a huge disappointment to him. Gilly was a great friend then and still is 20 years on."

After promotion was achieved, Pears continued to give great service. "After Bruce left, Colin Todd kept faith with me and then Lennie Lawrence helped get me into the England squad. Lennie was good for me and gave me great confidence, but when Bryan Robson arrived it changed. I was injured pre-season but the atmosphere was strange. He wanted his own people in and bought Alan Miller, who I didn't think was better than me. But he was younger and it was the manager's choice. It ended up as my final season at Boro and my testimonial game was a big boost for me financially.

"Unlike players these days who give the cash away, I needed the money to set me up for my life after football and bought a children's nursery business with the cash."

Time moves on and Pears is back in the goalkeeping trade. "I coach the young keepers from nine up to 18 years and although the nursery business has been sold, I also enjoy buying and selling properties. My two boys, Bradley, who is 14, and Aynsley, eight, both want to be goalkeepers and I wouldn't stand in their way."

Clearly for Pears though, Ayresome Park still retains its magic. "I think it's sad that the ground is no longer there and I drive past the site on my way to the Riverside remembering the good times. I also hold the record for scoring the final goal at Ayresome when I converted a penalty in my testimonial. That's not a bad record for a keeper!"

5. Gary Parkinson: Number 5

Born: Thornaby January 10 1968

From: Everton FC YTS Scheme

Season 1986-87: 58 appearances

Current Occupation: Head of Youth with Blackpool Football Club

Numbers can be deceptive. Gary Parkinson wore the number five shirt throughout season '86-'87 but never played at centre-half. He was the enthusiastic right-back of the side and even now has the same love for football he brought to the team at Ayresome Park twenty years ago.

We agreed to meet at the Tickled Trout, a hotel just outside Preston close to the M6. Parky was a bit late, one of the young players he coached had come down with flu and he was anxious that the bug didn't spread among the rest of the lads and that the right medication was taken to comply with football's strict drug taking restrictions.

As I waited for him to arrive I checked the records again for season '86-'87. Gary made his debut on the opening day against Port Vale on August 23 and went on to play 78 first team games on the bounce until he missed a goalless draw at Leicester on December 5 1987. In total, in two promotion seasons he made 101 first team starts. Clearly bugs avoided contact with Gary.

Delighted to be back in the game, Gary took up his role at Blackpool just a few weeks before our get together. But while he may be a citizen of the north-west his love affair with the Boro still endures.

Surprisingly for a full-back, his first hero was a winger. "Terry Cochrane was my idol along with the likes of Mark Proctor, Craig Johnston, Dave Hodgson and Dave Armstrong. They were mainly lads who had come through the youth set up, which would be the same for us in '86. I was always in the Holgate End, sometimes trying to get a squeeze in, but most of the time going with my dad. I just remember the atmosphere, especially for night matches. With the floodlights on it was a magical place and I would go home and dream about playing at Ayresome."

Most players have to put up with rejection at some stage in their careers and this was brought home early on. "I went to St Patrick's School in Thornaby and was asked to go to Boro for a trial, but they didn't think I was good enough so I travelled all over. I went to Southampton, Chelsea and Manchester City before eventually Everton offered me a YTS apprenticeship. I was only young and got homesick. Lee Turnbull was at Goodison with me but I couldn't settle and even though they offered a one-year YTS and a one-year full apprenticeship, I came home.

"Darlington wanted me to sign and they made a real fuss of me but when Boro scout Barry Geldart offered me a chance to train with my hometown club, I jumped at it and thankfully Willie Maddren followed it up with a two-year YTS. I will always be grateful to Willie."

After Willie Maddren came Bruce Rioch and the dramatic events of the summer of '86. "In one sense I was okay. Remember the YTS scheme was government funded, so Lee Turnbull, Stuart Ripley and I still received our money, but the older players were finding it a struggle. The worst day came at Longlands College. Bruce and Gary Pallister had a confrontation and training stopped. Players were not getting paid and were demotivated and I thought the club could die.

"It was down to Bruce, though, that the team pulled back together and we carried on training anywhere we could. We used to climb over the wall at Hutton Road to get on to the pitches and we'd throw our jumpers down anywhere from Clairville Common to Billingham Synthonia. I used to ride on my bike from Thornaby, where I lived with mam and dad, to wherever we were training. I couldn't afford to get on a bus as the club weren't paying any expenses. So that was my day, cycle in, clean the boots, bike back home. It wasn't a chore to me, it was a way of getting extra fitness, but I couldn't imagine the young lads at Blackpool or anywhere else for that matter putting up with that today."

The training sessions were also football master classes. "We might not have had a training ground but just look at the coaching staff: Bruce Rioch, Colin Todd, David Nish, Brian Little, Eddie Gray, all former stars of the game and they taught us so much. Mind, we could never beat the staff in five-a-sides!"

Before the interview, I'd heard all the rumours from ex-players that Parky was the 'whipping boy' and Bruce used to grab him by the throat if he made a mistake. The truth comes from the man himself. "Look, Bruce was a disciplinarian, and if he said 'jump' it was just a case of 'how high?'. But I had a great relationship with him. I remember no matter how desperate the times may have been, every morning you got the same question. 'How are you today?' The answer had to be, 'I feel fantastic, brilliant, a million dollars Bruce'. Anything other than that and it was in his office for a bollocking. You might be feeling a bit tired or below par but no excuse, you had to be up for training.

"Bruce was also keen to keep your feet on the ground. When I got in the team I thought any minute now someone will take my place. But I played 20 then 30 then 40 games on the bounce and thought 'I'm in here'. Then he pulled me to one side saying, 'Gary, you might be thinking about buying a car soon - no sports cars though, I don't want to see you arriving for training in anything flash'. It was just his way of keeping your feet on the ground.

"All I know was that he was the right boss for us that summer and we had a great desire to do well for him and for the town. A few years later we were training at Maiden Castle, near Durham, and when the news came out that he'd been sacked, half the lads were in tears. The bubble might have burst but he had given us such great times."

Season '86-'87 saw Boro string some great results together. "It began against Port Vale on my debut. I must be the only player to have made his home debut 'away', as we played at Hartlepool. After that match we went nine league games without defeat, winning six, and in the run-in we won eight and drew one of the last nine. The back four and the keeper were the same week in week out - Pears, Parkinson, Mowbray, Pallister and Cooper. I know fans say I was the weak link, but I don't mind that looking at the company I was in. Pearsy, great keeper, should have played for England. Mowbray, terrific leader, and got a transfer eventually to Celtic. Pallister, winning titles at Manchester United, then Coops becoming an England international. I don't mind being the weak link for that lot!"

Socially, the players mixed in a way that would be frowned upon today. "A few of us would go to Macmillans after a game and then on to Fatso's for a meal, but it was just the way we liked it, mingling with the fans and just being part of the community."

The memories remain vivid. "After we won promotion in '86-'87 we did it again the following season. I look back on the play-off with Chelsea and remember the bus getting bombarded by their fans. I was worrying about my family while I was on the pitch however Mogga and Pally kept their attacks out, helping us to get promotion to the equivalent of the Premier League. On the way back, the club said we could go anywhere we wanted, money no object, and instead of a posh restaurant we stopped off at a fish and chip shop and enjoyed our meal with the fans. That summed the spirit up. I had great pride in playing at Wembley in the ZDS Cup final for Boro in 1990 and I've kept all the photos at home."

Time ran out for Gary at the Boro under Lennie Lawrence. "He just wanted to bring in his own players. He thought I possibly had been there too long, so I rang Bruce and he offered me a chance at Bolton. I was devastated to leave, I never wanted to go.

"I had some great times after Boro, scoring the winning goal in the play-off final for Burnley at Wembley, playing twice at the Millennium Stadium and picking up PFA awards, but nothing ever matched my time at Boro. I still go back to the area and I was able to show my eldest lad, who is now 13, Ayresome Park before it was knocked down. But my two daughters were too young and didn't get to see where I played."

We finished our tea and his mobile phone rang. It was another youth player in need of advice. Before he left Gary had a final thought on the Boro of twenty years before. "I can still remember running out, the Holgate crammed full and shouting at Mogga to win the toss so we could attack the East End, which was usually empty in the first half, and we could then charge towards the Holgate in the second half. For a time we thought we were unbeatable. It was the greatest time of my life."

As I arrived back in Middlesbrough, a text message came from Gary. "Thanks for meeting today and going through some memories. It was brilliant and brought back some great times. I was very lucky to be part of such a brilliant time, Parky."

That's Gary Parkinson. Top man, and far from the weakest link.

6. Colin Cooper: Number 3

Born: Sedgefield February 28 1967

From: Juniors in 1984

Season 1986-87: 58 appearances

Current Occupation: Reserve team manager with Middlesbrough FC

Rockliffe Park is nestled in rolling countryside by the banks of the Tees on the borders of South Durham and North Yorkshire. It's where I met up with Colin one Friday afternoon just after he finished a session in the gym at Boro's state-of-the-art training facility.

Downstream around 15 miles, the Tees rolls under the Transporter Bridge, one of Middlesbrough's most famous landmarks, on its way to meeting the North Sea at Teesmouth.

Of course, it meanders past the Riverside Stadium, which is a far cry from Ayresome Park, but not as diametrically opposed as Rockliffe is to Hutton Road, Boro's old training ground a couple of miles south of the town centre.

In 1986 even that was out of bounds and Cooper recalls the day in the summer of that year when they reported back for training at Ayresome Park.

"I remember turning up and being told we weren't allowed in. We hung around for a bit and were eventually allowed in to get some kit which was still there. We then disappeared off somewhere and that was the scene for most of the summer. We would turn up, get kit, get changed and get out, we weren't allowed to stay in the ground. Bruce would direct us to where we had been given permission to train that day.

"Sometimes it was Marske Hills, sometimes on the beach at Redcar, Stewart Park, Albert Park or Kirklevington Young Offenders Institute."

Cooper was one of the younger members of a young squad and he admits that summer was demanding. "I'd just made my breakthrough and didn't really know what the future held, none of us did. Some players had the chance to leave and I wasn't one of them. I think Gary Hamilton and Peter Beagrie and one or two others had. Peter was the only one to leave and I can say honestly that it was nothing malicious with him. I think he was like me, scared. Scared for the future, scared of what might happen to us, having just made our breakthrough in football. I don't bear any ill feeling to Peter for going because none of us knew what was happening. But I think he might regret not being a part of the group which survived.

"We would turn up on a Thursday or Friday at the town hall and get paid off the liquidators. I remember asking Barry Geldart the chief scout at the time what was going on, what was happening? I'd played around 10 games, some of the lads had played more, some less, but I didn't know if I would have to go on trial somewhere having spent two and half years bedding myself in.

"I'd just got my first professional contract and this happened, so yes, I was certainly frightened. Barry said, 'If the worst comes to the worst then you'll be okay, you'll get another club'. But you wonder, of course you wonder. I suppose that's why I turned out to be a defender because I always concentrate on the negatives, the worst-case scenario."

Frantic work behind the scenes by a dedicated group was to overcome the odds and allay Cooper's pessimism. He now looks back on what he says was a turning point in the 130-year history of the club.

"I think the summer of '86 was a lucky summer for the football club in many ways.

"The local pride thing helped. Not only had we been given a chance, we had been given a chance at a club where we all wanted to succeed, and sometimes in football that just doesn't happen. We were all aiming for the same cause and that helped. There was a bit of fear factor in us all. We were a fairly talented bunch of youngsters thrown together with a smattering of experience and we pulled each other through, right through the season. We had to, there was no choice. We knuckled down and got on with it and as a club and as players, we got lucky.

"I've said before and I'll say it again, without those lads from '86, Middlesbrough Football Club as we now know it wouldn't exist."

When any model is being assembled it needs glue to keep it together. The glue in '86 was Bruce Rioch. Cooper's admiration for the former Scottish international still shines as brightly now with Cooper as it did 20 years ago.

"As a group of young professionals I think we were very lucky to have Bruce. He brought all the personal issues into line, discipline, your shape, attitude, your willingness to work hard for yourself and the team and the club and to make you feel something for the club you were playing for. Much of what I learned from Bruce I live by today. Appearance, my own personal discipline, my attitude, stuff like that, these are things I learned off him and I think if you take the positives from everyone you ever work under, you won't go far wrong."

Alongside Bruce was Colin Todd, a tough-as-teak defender with a human touch. "Much of the defending I used throughout my career I learned from Toddy," admits Coops.

"Toddy was more one of the lads at that point, but what I learned from him was the art of defending. I had got in the side the previous season as a midfielder, but we shuffled around during the summer and I ended up at left full-back, what I learned back then still sticks in the mind today.

"Toddy was the link. Every club has them, the manager has to draw a line and people like Toddy are the link between him and the dressing room. I saw him at a game when Boro played Chelsea. He was with his young grandson getting Frank Lampard's autograph. We still had time for chitchat for 15 minutes and we rolled the clock back."

It wasn't all plain sailing through the season. Yes, it ended successfully. Yes there were times when it looked as though good runs would never end. But there were occasions when all didn't go to plan.

"We played crap at times, we played some good football at times and we dug out results," admits Cooper. "The one which sticks out in my mind was the away game at Newport County. It was the coldest, wettest of days and there was hardly anybody in the ground. Tony Mowbray scored the winner in the 89th minute - I think that epitomised that season. We all played our part, every single one of us played our part during that season.

"Through goodwill and good grace, and some cracking coaching from Bruce and Toddy, we got to where we wanted, and that was out of that division quickly."

Momentum built throughout that season, not just on the pitch but off it as well. "The football team is the focus of the town. It still is - if the team win on a Saturday people go to work happy on a Monday. We used to spend time in the town on a Saturday night mixing with the fans. We were young lads, we went out to bars and clubs and mixed. You knew that they would have a good night and go to work happy on the Monday if they at least knew we had given everything for their club.

"Pearsy kept 32 clean sheets that season, Bernie and Archie got goals, others chipped in with what they could do. We knew that on our day we were a good, honest side who could defend, but that was a team thing. Then we would probably rely on Bernie at the other end! But he would be the first to admit it was a team thing. With one element missing we would have struggled, with two missing we would have struggled badly, but no elements were missing.

"There are too many times over the years that players have come who have no feeling at all and we're now looking for the right kind of people to bring in. You can never roll the clock back, but if you can get people who want to do well for the club and each other as we had then, then you're heading in the right direction."

In time Cooper's career with Middlesbrough would go stale. A move to Millwall was followed by a return north to Nottingham and eventually back to where it all started. Well almost. Ayresome Park had been flattened for three years by the time he returned to Teesside.

"I personally felt my career was on a downward spiral," he admits. "The team had started to move on. Big Pally had gone to Manchester United, and I just felt I didn't know where my career was going. I'll be honest, if I hadn't moved on I have no idea where I would have ended up or what I would have been doing.

"I certainly wouldn't be where I am now, I certainly wouldn't have played for England and I certainly wouldn't have played in the Premier League for two thirds of my career. I was in a massive comfort zone and I was allowed to be in a massive comfort zone. I missed large parts of two seasons with a broken foot and other injuries. When I started to play again it was at right-back and I turned into a stroppy little kid who threw his toys out of the pram from time to time because I didn't like where I was playing.

"It's only in recent years I realise how good the move was for me. Lennie Lawrence has kindly said that he feels it was the worst piece of business he ever did at Middlesbrough in letting me go, but had I stayed I would have drifted, maybe gone into the lower leagues or even out of the game – my career was on a downward spiral.

"The move to Millwall with Bruce gave me the kick up the arse I needed. There were no highs and no lows, but a lot of in-betweens. It didn't work out for Bruce there, but I was lucky in that big Mick McCarthy came in and asked me to play centre-half and that changed my career. It started to go in the right direction again."

Two years in south-east London came to an end. "It was a difficult move, but another challenge, so we upped sticks from Kent and moved to Nottinghamshire, where I had five enjoyable years."

They were followed by a return home.

"Dave Bassett came in to help Stuart Pearce who had been given the caretaker's role after Frank Clark had left Nottingham Forest. We got relegated and Stuart left, with a little bit of help from Bassett, I believe. Mr Bassett tried to get me out of the club as well. He told me I would never play for Forest again as long as he was manager. I was club captain and not ready to leave, and I dug my heels in.

"After a poor start to the season changes were made and I got my place back. We went on a cracking run and won the championship, closely followed by the Boro."

A call in the summer from assistant manager Viv Anderson was to result in Cooper's career completing a full circle.

"When I spoke to him he told me Bryan Robson wanted to sign players of an ilk that would make sure that when Middlesbrough got promoted this time, they wouldn't get relegated. Robson had signed some special players, especially Juninho and Ravanelli, but others like Gianluca Festa, who was terrific for the club, Paul Merson, Emerson. Players like that coming to Middlesbrough was fantastic, but he wanted to make sure Boro stopped being a yo-yo club. He brought me back, he brought Pally back, Andy Townsend was here, Gazza was here, so too were Dean Gordon, Robbie Mustoe, Curtis Fleming and Steve Vickers. The backbone of the side and the big star of that season was Hamilton Ricard.

"Bryan wanted steel in the side. The years of free-scoring and relegation he wanted to end. He wanted a team who could dig in and keep clean sheets, survive in the Premiership and to build from there. So when the call came it was a case of how quickly I could get up the motorway. It was a great move for my family as well."

Tragedy struck in 2002 when the Coopers lost their two-year-old son Finlay. But the football community which knows Colin and hundreds who don't, rallied round and support from them, and from his remarkably resilient wife Julie, made sure that a man with a deep passion for the good things in the game stayed in it to help others live values forged in the summer of '86.

We could have talked for hours, Colin speaks from the heart with an infectious love of football and common decency and it would be easy to listen all day.

"What happened back in '86 was just right. Every single person who played in that team and everyone who helped the club survive should give themselves a pat on the back. The chairman has since had a completely different vision and the club we are part of now is so completely removed from that of '86, it's impossible to imagine.

"I walked off the training pitch with Stephen Pears the other day and said what a long time 20 years was. It is in someone's life, but maybe not in the life of a football club. But what a chunk it's been in Boro's existence.

"To go from where we were in the summer of '86 to where we are now is, I think, nothing short of phenomenal.

"Twenty years is a long time, but I'd like to think that what we do really remember is each other, and a lot of those friendships we built up are still pretty strong today."

Colin Cooper, one of life's decent guys.

7. Alan Kernaghan: Number 10

Born: Otley April 25 1967

From: Signed professional forms in 1985

Season 1986-87: 14 appearances, plus seven as non-playing sub. One goal.

Current Occupation: In between managerial positions.

I had enjoyed a good run up to Edinburgh early one Monday morning, timing the run to avoid the horrendous traffic which plagues the west of Newcastle and the southern tip of Scotland's capital city every day.

The day got even better when breakfast, in the form of two huge cups of coffee, was bought by Alan Kernaghan.

As we settled into a seat outside Costa Coffee in the Gyle Shopping Centre, situated in an out of town retail and business park much like many other, a few miles to the west of Auld Reekie, big Al admitted that his memories of the summer of '86 began pretty early.

"I remember on the coach back from being relegated at Shrewsbury in the final game of the previous season, saying to coach Danny Bergara, 'I'm now a third division player'. He said, 'No you're not, you're a good player in the wrong division'."

Kerny needed confidence - all the players did - and those words helped.

Despite being born in Otley, not far from Bradford, in West Yorkshire, Kernaghan's roots are in the country he would go on to represent on the international stage, Ireland.

"I went home that summer and didn't really think about the next season that much. It was only when I came back I realised that there was something wrong. Even then it seemed reasonably normal at first, but then we started to go training.

"Hutton Road was in a mess, the club didn't have any money to fund its upkeep and we weren't allowed to use Ayresome Park. We did a lot at Billingham Synthonia and out and about at some of the local parks. We played games against the likes of Norton and Stockton I think - I scored a hat-trick do you believe? One was a penalty and one of the others an overhead kick. So on the field it wasn't too bad.

"But we weren't getting paid, I was in digs and the landladies weren't getting paid. The club used to use the Medhurst Hotel, that was a fantastic place where about 20 lads stayed, but had sold it and I had stayed in Oxford Road and other places in and around the Linthorpe area. Wherever we were, the landladies weren't getting paid.

"The first port of call when you are a young lad in need of money is your Mam and Dad, and I used to get some sent over. But when the club sorted the financial position out I got paid around eight weeks' wages and felt like a millionaire!"

Kernaghan says that a bond which would last for two decades was unknowingly being forged, though one or two left the club and he admits he might have.

"I don't know what I would have done had there been an offer for me as there were for other players, but there wasn't one so that situation never arose. It was different for me than for some of the others. I was 18 or 19 with no commitments, the ones who left had, and I don't blame them for jumping ship. But I'm delighted I stayed. The spirit just grew and grew and grew.

"Bruce was the leader. He and Toddy used to keep us informed as best they could. Mogga was a funny one, you know. He wasn't outspoken in the changing room, but his leadership came from what he did on the pitch."

When the season eventually got underway, Kernaghan admits that while relief was the underlying emotion, there was a pressing need to concentrate on a new style of play the team were trying to perfect.

"We'd moved away from being the 'up and at 'em' style and jackets for goalposts sort of outfit, to one which was trying to play decent football. We now had a structure of what we wanted to do and what our role in the team was. It wasn't always like that. In fact, I don't think any of the lads who were there had had that kind of structure, but it was pretty clear it was going to work.

"I think I played in the first game because Gary Pallister was suspended after being sent-off at Shrewsbury, but I was versatile and was asked to play at centre-forward. I remember being embarrassed when completely missing the ball when attempting to score from a Stuart Ripley cross. Maybe if I'd had a bit of the 'Bernie' inside of me it would have been better. Maybe technically I might have been a better player than Bernie, but he had a goalscoring instinct which I never had, that's what hindered me as a striker and that was evident that day.

"I played up front in that first game. Bernie was out on the left, which he detested. He claimed everything went down the right, that no-one would pass to him and that no-one liked him! It was always a joke to us."

The social scene was important to the players during those days. It helped bond the players as a team and the team with their fans.

"We used to go to the Madison in Middlesbrough town centre and Billy Paul's, which was just underneath it, but that was just about it, though some of the lads used to go to The Mall, which had just started up in Stockton.

"Everyone got on well, on and off the pitch and I'm sure, no, I know that helped."

It was that spirit which helped get the season off to a good start and subsequently gather momentum.

"I remember when we finally got to train on Ayresome Park for the first time that summer, it was fantastic. The ball just rolled and rolled and we hit it off straight away. I remember Bruce being interviewed on the TV and talking about 'rallying the troops' - he usually had some army quotation. We didn't need rallying, the spirit was good, but he organised us so well.

"We had characters in that dressing room, like Hammy, who was in the kindest sense an idiot with the way he used to go on. Only since I have lived in Scotland, which has been for eight years now, have I realised that's the way a lot of Scots are in the dressing room and that's why they do so well in the game. They're not scared of anybody and play with an unbelievable freedom and Hammy was that way.

"Stuart Ripley is very intelligent, but had absolutely no common sense at all. I remember when he was an apprentice he went out to buy his lunch - there were no canteens or restaurants in those days - coming back with a frozen chicken leg which he tried to eat straight away. He'll probably kill me for saying so, but one of his nicknames was Gripper Stebson after a bully character in Grange Hill. He was quiet most of the time but he had a temper and when he lost it, he lost it big style. Rippers probably had more O Levels than the rest of us put together, but he was as daft as a brush.

“I used to room with him and many a night when I was trying to get to sleep, all I could here was him reciting his French studies. Or I’d be sat watching the TV and he’d be studying.”

So what did Kerny make of Bruce?

“He was very regimental and maybe he was very lucky that we were at such a young age that he could not so much bully us, but push us in the direction where we wanted to go. He ruled some by fear, he did with me. Others, like Mogga, Coops and Pearsy, he would leave pretty much to get on with things, but I called him ‘Gadaffi’ and I don’t think I was alone. I think he always had it in for me. He was always on my case and it’s not until much later that you realise he’s doing it with the best intentions. It wasn’t until he left that I realised how good he was.

“I think Bolton Wanderers are where they are these days because of what Bruce did for them with the likes of Jason McAteer, Alan Stubbs and Alan Thompson, who all went on to have great careers. I thought he was fantastic. I hated him at the time, but he was really good.”

Alan left Middlesbrough in 1993, but not before captaining the side and scoring a hat-trick at Blackburn. “I heard later it kept Bruce in the job.

“I moved to Manchester City, and while it wasn’t the worst move I could have made, it wasn’t far from it. I just joined the wrong club at the wrong time. Financially it was very good at the time. When I joined Peter Swales was just being removed as chairman. All the fans were concerned about was getting him out and Franny Lee in and not about the football. From being at a team which truly was a team, I went to a side full of individuals who were doing their own thing, and I found it hard to cope with, to tell the truth. I regret it now. I think a lot of it was down to the club, but some of it was down to me not having a strong enough character to deal with it and be myself.”

Loan deals followed to Bolton, managed by Rioch, and St Johnstone where Paul Sturrock was in charge. “It was just a case of getting away from Manchester City. Frank Clark was City manager at the time and asked if I wanted to go. I asked him where it was. He said, ‘Scottish Premier League’. I had meant geographically! I found out and remembered playing there with Boro.

“I moved straight away and had a great time. The football there put a smile back on my face. We qualified for Europe, reached a Scottish Cup final and a semi-final. It was great.

“Injuries became the bane of my life, though. I had three operations on a pelvic problem which it turned out I didn't need. I came to the end of my contract there, wasn't offered another one and went to play for Brechin for three months. The chance then came to go to Clyde as player-coach. That was strange as half the team were full-time and half part-time. The management team left, I put my hat into the ring, got the job and for two-and-a-half years had a pretty successful time.

"From there I went to Livingston as player-coach with a good friend Allan Preston, but it didn't work out and I was sacked. I went to play for half a season at Falkirk, then got the chance to be youth team coach there and from there the chance came to manage Dundee in September 2005. I found the club in disarray. They had just been relegated and the situation was not dissimilar to that which the Boro had been in all those years ago in terms of going through administration. They had moved on some players like Claudio Caniggia and Fabrizio Ravanelli, fantastic players, but they were on astronomical wages.

"Despite all the problems we had we still managed to reach the semi-final of the Scottish Cup in April, but I was sacked soon after. I had seen it coming after a bad run in the league and Alex Rae, who took over, had the same problems in trying to move players on and bring in others on lower wages just to keep the club going."

The shoppers were beginning to mass in greater numbers as lunchtime approached. Had we really been talking that long? But before Alan goes to the nearby airport to pick up his wife after her holiday in India, he reflects: "I remember when I left Middlesbrough, Steve Gibson said, 'Don't sign anything until you've spoken to me'. I never did speak to him and I regret that.

"I met him recently. A more down to earth, salt of the earth person you couldn't wish to meet. I look back with enormous pleasure at my time with Middlesbrough. It wasn't all good, but even though I'm not from the area, I spent 10 years there and sometimes still think of it as home."

8. Gary Pallister: Number 6

Born: Ramsgate June 30 1965

From: Billingham Town

Season 1986-87: 56 appearances, one goal

Current Occupation: Freelance media broadcaster (BBC, Sky, Channel 5) and property developer.

Away from the boundaries of Teesside, if you mention the name Gary Pallister to football fans they will probably link it with Manchester United. There, in a glittering career, he made more than 400 appearances, winning four Premier League titles, lifting the FA Cup on three occasions and also threw in for good measure a League Cup and a European Cup Winners Cup.

Quite simply, Pally was one of the best defenders of his generation, earning 22 England caps. Sir Alex Ferguson paid him the highest compliment by including him in his greatest-ever Manchester United line up.

In retirement he is surrounded by evidence of a footballer made good, a beautiful home overlooking Yarm and property interests in nearby Middlesbrough.

Nevertheless, his football roots are firmly in the Boro. He was originally given a trial by Malcolm Allison but played only one reserve game before being released. Willie Maddren was coach under Allison and kept in touch with Pally's progress. When he became boss, he signed the young defender.

It was hardly a headline-making deal. Due to Boro's financial problems, he was only taken on when local businessman, Dick Corden, agreed to pay his modest wage of £50 a week.

At the end of a hugely-successful first spell at the Boro, Pally would attract a then record-breaking transfer fee to set up the move to Old Trafford. But in November 1984, his club Billingham Town didn't even receive a fee for him. Instead they were given a set of strips, with some footballs thrown in for good measure.

It was a struggle at first and he was loaned out to Darlington before Maddren - once a stylish defender himself - gave him his debut.

As Gary answered the intercom and the security gates were about to open I wondered if twenty years on the events of 1986 would even register after the glory years at United and international caps for England. But thankfully, as I was about to find out, that season still evokes great pride in what was achieved from the ashes of liquidation.

Before the interview I viewed some old footage of the players arriving at the Victoria Ground, Hartlepool, for the first game. Amongst the players is Pally, but he was suspended for an incident that still preys on his mind. "The final game of the previous season was at Shrewsbury. We ended up relegated and I was sent off for a professional foul - but I definitely played the ball!

"After the match I felt more to blame than anyone as we were back in the match when I was shown the red card, then we ended up defeated and relegated. It wasn't the way I wanted my first full season with the club to end up and you could tell from the mood that it was going to be a difficult summer."

The match at Gay Meadow had ended badly for player and club but as Pally set off on holiday, nothing could prepare him for what would happen next: "I went to Tenerife for a couple of weeks with my girlfriend and after a few days phoned home. Mam answered and said, 'Looks like you're out of a job son!' I couldn't believe what I was hearing. 'The club's gone bust, it's in liquidation and it could be the end.' I knew things were bad. After all, a club that's in good shape doesn't need someone to pay me £50-a-week. But you always thought football clubs muddled through. And now here I was, holiday ruined, as my mind kept on drifting to what on earth was I going to do now."

Initially the answer was to return to some form of training at Boro. "It was embarrassing. We trained anywhere and just threw our jackets on the floor for goalposts. It was just like being back at school."

As the crisis deepened, players began to fear the worst and Crystal Palace were prepared to throw Pally a lifeline. But as Steve Gibson recalls the involvement of Palace and, in particular, their chairman Ron Noades, left a sour taste. "Noades was a member of the Football League Management Committee. The Football League were asking us to do things which were unreasonable and we found out that Ron Noades had our players, Gary Pallister and Brian Laws, at Selhurst Park telling them that if Middlesbrough Football Club went out of business, they'd be interested in signing them. Talk about self-interest! He later wrote in Four Four Two magazine how he had been offered Gary Pallister by the receivers for £35,000 but he'd refused because he didn't want to do any damage to Middlesbrough Football Club. That's not the way it happened."

However Pallister was a young footballer deeply concerned about his future and remembers the visit to London well. "I went down there and met Steve Coppell, then Palace manager, and Ron Noades. Steve broke the ice by mentioning that they had a good kid who they had just taken from non-league who would score the goals - his name was Ian Wright. I went to the meeting with my dad but I knew life in London wasn't for me and I really went just to avoid being ignorant. I just hoped Boro would be okay and that I could stay on Teesside. Other lads like Don O'Riordan left, but it was different for Don, he had a family to support and I was just a kid with no commitments."

Mention of the Pallister-Rioch relationship initially brings only laughter from Gary. "I had a lot of issues with Bruce later in my career and I fell out with him that summer when he sent me home from training. He couldn't fine me, though, because I wasn't being paid anyway. It was crazy.

"Despite our personal problems, I have to admit he was the ideal man at that time to keep us all bonded together. When the season started we played a brand of passing, attractive football with the emphasis on entertaining the fans and that was all down to Bruce.

"We had a great keeper in Stephen Pears, who would go on to be one of the best in the country, Cooper and Parkinson as full-backs, Parky was still learning and could be a bit raw, but attacking he gave us options and just in front were Gary Hamilton and Brian Laws. The side had a great work ethic. I found out later at United you can have class players like Giggs, Beckham and Kanchelskis, but they still have to do the dirty work and get back and tuck in. If you don't, the back four are in trouble. Laws and Hamilton did that job for us."

The heart of the defence that in thirteen games from March 17 until the end of the season kept 10 clean sheets to win promotion was Pallister and Tony Mowbray. "Our partnership was similar to the one I enjoyed with Steve Bruce at United. Neither player had great pace, if they had they would have won loads of England caps, but they put their heads where others wouldn't put their boots and timed tackles to perfection. At Ayresome, Mogga was a great organiser on the pitch and a terrific captain. Away from the ground we mixed socially but he wasn't a big drinker - perhaps a glass of wine or a beer on a night out."

Back then those nights out could still be enjoyed with fans, as the players were part of the community. "I was on £350 per week basic and enjoyed nights in Bentley's nightclub in Stockton, or sometimes the Madison in the Boro. All the fans were saying it was like a breath of fresh air that season after all the problems in previous years, with local youngsters playing for the team, and in a way it's similar today with the likes of Cattermole, Downing, McMahon, all local lads playing for the club."

Celebrations came after promotion was clinched against Wigan. "We passed our way out of that division, playing some great stuff, but that night we battered them but just couldn't get a goal. If we had scored once we probably would have got five or six. When the whistle went and we had gone up it was fantastic - cans of beer (no champagne!), jumping in the bath and just great pride that we had achieved promotion with, basically, just a bunch of kids. I remember standing in the directors' box trying to take it all in. In sport, occasions like that are few and far between. There was just a great feeling of pride."

So among all the medals and titles, where does a Division Three runners-up medal in 1987 actually rank? "In terms of buzz and feeling, standing on the edge of the directors' box at Ayresome was same as winning the European Cup Winners Cup with United against Barcelona. Celebrating that night in the Boro was something I never wanted to end, it was that good."

Sadly, all good things come to an end. Today, Gary is much in demand for media work and has two young daughters to keep him busy. Add in his new found interest in property development, plus the need to keep the golf handicap down and beat his former team-mates at tennis, and he's a busy man!

But like most ex-pros, it's the dressing room banter that he misses the most. "I played in the Match on Sky, Celebrities v Ex-Pros, and the crack with Peter Reid, John Barnes and Ian Rush was brilliant, and at United they got the FA Cup-winning side of 1990 back together, with Robbo, Brucie and McClair, and it was just as if we had never been away."

Before I left examined his medals, signed shirts, photos of great days with England and I thought how far he had come from being part of a deal that gave a non-league club a few shirts and a few footballs. The conversation comes back to 1986. "I felt I was part of an amazing chapter in the history of the Boro. After liquidation the team restored pride in the town. My mam and dad were great Boro fans and it was terrific to give them something back."

9. Gary Gill: Number 10

Born: Middlesbrough November 28 1964

From: Juniors in 1981

Season 1986-87: 45 appearances, plus three as unused substitute. Two goals

Current Occupation: Northern executive for Pepe Jeans and football correspondent for BBC Radio Cleveland.

I always say that Gary Gill summarises the game better than most people I know. Such is his understanding of tactics and players, it is perhaps something of a surprise that a career in management or coaching hasn't been undertaken.

The dressing room's loss is the BBC's gain and it somehow seemed appropriate that I caught up with Gary shortly before he went on air to co-commentate with Paul Addison as part of BBC Radio Cleveland's coverage of Boro's game at Bolton.

When Gill was a player, Bolton v Boro was played at either Ayresome or Burnden Park. Today it's the Reebok or the Riverside, a far cry from 1986 as he recalls.

"We knew the club was in trouble, but Bruce Rioch did his best to deflect at lot of that away from us, allowing us to get on with what we could when we could. But we knew we were in trouble when we didn't have a training pitch and we got together pretty much anywhere which was big enough for 16 or so players.

"I know now that it was very close as to whether we survived or not, but back then I didn't think we would go out of business. I just didn't think it would happen, I don't know why. I just didn't think a club like ours could fold, I genuinely believed that."

Despite the underlying confidence of Gill and most of his team mates, players were allowed to leave if certain financial conditions weren't met by the consortium – if they hadn't been paid for six weeks the Football League decreed that they were allowed to move elsewhere. But for Gill, that was never an option.

"It wasn't a difficult choice for me. I know Peter Beagrie left and I don't blame him for that, he hadn't been paid for six weeks. As far I was concerned I was sticking where I was, waiting to get a chance to start the season and do my bit for the team.

"What was important for the future was the team spirit engendered there and then that summer. What was going on was far from great, but it helped create a team spirit which was exceptionally special.

"There wasn't a bad apple among us, everybody had their role to play, their bit to offer and a group of predominantly local lads just got on so well. We took it seriously, by golly we did, we didn't hold back, but we had a great time and that helped us on the pitch."

The opening game at Hartlepool, well chronicled elsewhere in this book, brings a smile to Gilly's face when the details are recalled. "We probably should have won that game, Archie had scored twice with goals we knew he wasn't capable of scoring! So why that happened we don't know. Yes, we were disappointed, but we were up and running.

"The next game took us to Wigan and we were battered in the first half, we couldn't work out how we were still 0-0 at half-time. But there were some soothing words from Bruce – and that wasn't a regular thing. And the belief we had running through that side that we could get something, not just from the second-half of that game but from the season, shone through. We went on to win 2-0 and I think that game epitomised our season. There was an assuredness, a calmness, a belief and some very, very good football. That result at Springfield Park, as much as any that season, got us on our way."

That match was the second in a nine-game unbeaten start to a Third Division season which might never have featured Middlesbrough.

Gilly isn't the only player to mention one game from later in the campaign with particular fondness. Although maybe fondness is the wrong word…

"Newport County played at Somerton Park in those days. As we went out to warm-up the November sky in South Wales darkened, hailstones rattled off the roofs and we went to make our way off the pitch. It was a horrible day, a terrible pitch, horrific. There were about 1,500 people in the ground, mainly Boro fans. Big Pally had his sleeves down over his hands and said, 'Bugger this lads, let's get back in'. The Newport lads, fair play to them, hadn't turned out at this stage, but Bruce had. He was coming out just as we decided to come off. Words to the effect that under no circumstances were we leaving that pitch were uttered from him and we dutifully trotted back out and continued our exercises!

"We went on to win that game with an 89th-minute diving header from Tony Mowbray after a hell of a battle – that summed us up."

But Boro could play as bit as well.

"We'd had games like Newport and Wigan, but we also had games like the one against Bournemouth, who were our championship rivals, where we beat them 4-0 at Ayresome with a performance which brought our biggest win of the season and had Bruce purring.

"We had good players and a management team which got the best out of us. Don't forget, in that team we had players who would go on to play international football. Good players, great coaching and team spirit which was like an extra man, plus the returning belief of the fans made for a pretty good mix."

Back then the players didn't have a long-term vision. "For me it was a case of, 'Who are we playing in the next game and is my name on the team sheet?'. It was a case of enjoying ourselves at the time. We played on the Saturday, had a few pints with each other and the fans on a Saturday night and went training on Monday, which was always bright and good.

"You couldn't take anything for granted. Yes, we had a small squad, but you had to perform or there would be changes and that kept you on your toes.

"Bruce was a fantastic coach. Some of the things he taught you, some of the things he put into your mind about how to play attacking football, which is what he loved, stayed with us forever. Educationally, he was phenomenal. Some of the sessions he put on just blew you away. We thought we knew a bit about football, but here we were looking at a guy who left you thinking, 'I've got so far to go before I even know a small part of what he does'. He taught you good things.

"His best sessions I felt were when he used to say, 'Right, how do we get at teams? How do we score goals? How do we play attacking football and make life difficult for them and in the process entertain the fans?' He didn't do it to entertain the fans, that was a by-product, but he had a belief which was infectious."

But management wasn't all about Bruce Rioch and Gary speaks with great respect about the role played by Colin Todd. "He was the funniest man in the dressing room that summer. When you had had a run-in with Bruce, which could happen from time to time, Toddy was there with his arm around you explaining everything. He was fantastic and the way they worked undoubtedly worked for us.

"We were taught to do things right. We socialised together and never stepped out of line. You had too much respect for your team mates who were your mates off the pitch as well. We used to hammer each other, Gary Hamilton was the chief architect in that. He was ruthlessly funny and made sure no-one was let-off, no-one got a chance to believe they were better than they were. There was no place in that dressing room for big time Charlies and there weren't any. Deep down we all wanted to do well for the team."

Gary recalls at this point that neither Alastair or I were immune from the occasional rebuke from Mr Rioch, but this is not the time or the place to invoke those memories thank you very much.

Despite their undoubted ability on the pitch, the Class of '86 will also be remembered for their haircuts. "Look, it was a fashion statement," says Gilly, laughing. "We were all young, and blonde spiky cuts were the fashion at the time. It was trendy and went down a treat. It worked, didn't it? We all had nice girlfriends!

"But I have to say there was one player who wished he hadn't been to the hairdressers. We went on an end-of-season tour to America, I can't remember whether it was at the end of this season or the next. Alan Kernaghan went for a perm and they left the rollers in too long and he came out with almost like an Afro! We played Seattle, which was Bruce's old club in America, and we lost. This was hugely embarrassing for him and gave him a chance to have a right old go at some things which he hadn't been happy with on tour – one of which was Kerny's haircut.

"In the dressing room afterwards he pointed to the person under the frizzy perm and said, 'And you, you will never play for this club again with a haircut like that', which led to Kerny afterwards buying some of the strongest waxy gel you could buy and spending the rest of the holiday putting stacks in trying to straighten it – he got hammered."

Eventually it was time to move on and after Rioch made it clear that he wanted Gill out, the parting of ways was inevitable.

"I had a fall-out with Bruce and I objected to him telling me which club I was going to join. Scunthorpe had put in an offer of £200,000 and I said I would talk to them but that at twenty-five years old I didn't see myself as a Scunthorpe player at that time of my career.

"I'd fallen out with him before, but he had gone on to make me captain in the 1989-90 season which was a great honour. But injuries had held me back. I had been playing some great football until a stack of injuries got in the way, although

I did play for 15 minutes with a broken leg! But that's because I'm an idiot and didn't realise at the time that I had fractured my fibia – although I still had to walk from the ground to the General Hospital. That tells you what it was like back then.

"I think Bruce would say he made some mistakes with me over a new contract. He wouldn't say so then, but maybe would now and I'll admit I didn't handle myself very well. In December 1989 I went Darlington. I didn't want to go as I thought it was a graveyard for ex-Boro players – no disrespect to Darlington, where I went on to have smashing time with great success. But I thought I was capable of playing at a higher level. I needed someone to put their arm around me and didn't want to take a chance with a manager I didn't know, so I went to play for Brian Little who had been part of the Boro's youth and reserve set-up.

"I could have earned more money by going to other clubs, but chose not to. It was funny to find out that Brian had adopted a lot of Bruce's training methods, but he was maybe better at that time in handling lots of different characters."

A back complaint ended Gary's professional career and after Darlington, he played semi-pro in Sweden, went coaching in America and was a community officer with the Boro, before making his mark in the fashion industry.

"I played for the local team in Sven Goran Eriksson's home town in Sweden and they were quite advanced," he recalls. "It was set in a forest on the edge of a lake with a pub which only opened for two hours on a Saturday. I think I once described it as the most beautiful open prison in the world!"

But it was the summer of '86 which, Gary concludes, helped shape him for life. "Bruce had a massive effect on my life, not all good, but many good things. I saw him not long ago and there was real warmth there. There was something special in '86. I think all who were involved will tell you that, even big Pally, who went on to win just about everything with Manchester United and play for England. I think that even he will say that his happiest times in football were back then."

10. Gary Hamilton: Number 9

Born: Glasgow December 27 1965

From: Professional terms May 1983

Season 1986-87: 51 appearances, including three as substitute. Eight goals

Current Occupation: Executive director/director of coaching McAllen Football Club, Texas, USA.

It has been a long journey from the streets of Glasgow to the Rio Grande. But life has always been full of twists and turns for Gary James Hamilton, with one common denominator throughout - his love for football.

As the phone rang, I wondered just how the years had treated Hammy, as some of the class of '86 had mentioned they had lost touch with him and believed he had suffered from illness.

So had the spark gone from the player who was the midfield dynamo of a side that made the leap from liquidation to the top flight?

I need not have worried, as despite the miles I could tell, even with a hint of an American accent, that Gary was at ease with himself after turning forty in December and enjoying his role coaching soccer to kids in the States.

The lifestyle is good as well. "Do you remember John Wayne?" was his first question and when I answered in the positive the reply came, "Well I live just five miles from the Mexican border and sometimes dip my feet and my beer in the Rio Grande - real western stuff."

The Wild West was also a term used to describe parts of Glasgow when he was growing up, but after leaving school to try to earn a professional contract at Middlesbrough, early impressions of the town were far from favourable. "I know some say Glasgow isn't the greatest place on earth but when I arrived on Teesside it was bleak to say the least. The snow was horrendous and the industrial landscape in a dark midwinter was hardly promising. However, the one thing I remember that never changed in all my time there was the warmth of the people. They were very special."

Despite the warmth from the terraces, the club was in decline. "My first season was after the club had been relegated from Division One and I think that experience had started the slide to the problems of '86. Something had to happen, the crowds were dwindling and the supporters were annoyed at the way the club was being run. I had sympathy with them - if I had been working 60 hours a week and then watched the crap we were serving up I don't think I would have turned up either. They were sickened off and the players at the time must take some responsibility for that.

"Just look what happened after Bruce Rioch sorted us out. We started to play entertaining football and won the fans back again."

The Rioch years were far off when, after making his debut coming on as sub for Colin Ross in an away game at Bolton in February 1983, Gary then helped Malcolm Allison's team avoid the drop. He scored a crucial goal in the final home game of the season as a 2-0 win over Crystal Palace secured Division Two football.

After flirting with relegation, the inevitable happened on May 3 1985 at Shrewsbury, as the team slipped into Division Three. "I ended up relegated and with six stitches in a head wound, but although we were upset at going down, the enormity of what was about to happen didn't dawn on us. When you are young, a bit stupid and naïve, you think that life as a footballer will go on forever and that someone with barrowloads of money will turn up and save the club. Life, as I have discovered, isn't like that, and reality for the team back then was about to bite hard."

After the defeat at Gay Meadow, Gary headed back to Scotland for the close season but with financial problems mounting on Teesside, other offers started to come in. "Lennie Lawrence spoke to me and invited me to The Valley, but although I liked Lennie I couldn't see myself living in London. While keeping my options open by sounding out clubs in Scotland, I decided to ride out the storm at Boro, hoping the club would survive which, thanks to the help of ICI and others, it did."

Middlesbrough's future on the pitch was down to a man who was sharing the Hamilton digs. "I was fortunate, or unfortunate, to be in with Bruce Rioch at Mrs Crombie's house on Acklam Road in Middlesbrough. Apart from being able to keep an eye on me, Bruce was obsessed with football. As a kid in Scotland I remembered him captaining the team at the World Cup in 1978. He had been a top player and the football chat was non stop. That's how I learned of his intention to help Boro at every level, and during that summer take any burden off the players and as manager carry it for them."

In the dressing room, a real team spirit was born. "Stuart Ripley was my best friend along with Colin Cooper, but my room-mate on away trips was Tony Mowbray. I don't remember how we ended up together as he was a straight-laced guy and I was the opposite, but we got on well and on the field it was a privilege to play with him. Tony brought on the players around him, none more so than Mr Pallister.

"The title of the fanzine *Fly Me To The Moon* was in tribute to him and some of the lads in the dressing room didn't like that as it was inferring that he was carrying us forward. Some took badly to it, but they were the stupid ones, as Tony Mowbray was one of the biggest legends ever to play for Middlesbrough Football Club."

Memories of season '86-'87 are a bit of a blur. "I can't remember too much, thank God, as it was a division to get out of quickly, you didn't want to hang around there. But one goal I scored against Fulham at Ayresome in a 3-0 win remains in the memory, it was the best volley I scored in my career. On the score-sheet that day was Bernie Slaven. He had a great partnership with Archie Stephens but how Archie didn't thump him I will never know, as he would battle all day and then Bernie would pop up with a hat-trick! But that was Bernie, and why he ended up playing for the Republic of Ireland and going to the World Cup with them."

Promotion though, is always an achievement irrespective of the division. "Before you rang," says Hammy, "I remembered that I still have the video of the promotion night against Wigan and that was the start of the push for promotion the following season. Bruce just used to get in your head, 'Let's go seven games undefeated'. Then he would set another target and before you knew it, it was Christmas and you were top of the league.

"We just failed to go up automatically and I went mad the day of the final game at home with Leicester City as it was a carnival before kick-off, with trophies ready to hand out at the final whistle. That was setting you up for a fall and we mightn't have heard of Gary McAllister before the match but we had 90 minutes later as he ran the show. We lost and ended in the play-offs, which was horrible.

"Bruce, though, showed his understanding of psychology. He hated gambling but ordered us to bring money in, as we were 3/1 for the play-offs. To the players it was amazing as we knew how much he disliked players thowing money at bookies. It was his way of saying he believed in us and when we went to the USA for a tour after promotion, he opened a suitcase full of cash and paid us in full."

Unfortunately, the Hamilton top-flight experience lasted only one season. "We were relegated at Sheffield Wednesday on the last day of the season, the only time we had been in the drop zone, and it was my final game for the club. I had injury problems, all the managers were great to me Bruce, Colin Todd, Lennie Lawrence, but I just couldn't play any more. And that's when it hits you, what are you going to do when all you ever wanted to do is taken away? Now I know that no-one can take away the fact I played and, as I have found out, there are more important things in life."

The big surprise was that America called. "I came over in the summer of '92 to coach at some soccer camps. In those days if you had a British accent you got a job, as they figured you must know something about the game! I went from Dallas to Houston, then ended up here, near the Rio Grande. At first I didn't like it but I have helped build up the club from 270 kids to 2,400. It's tough in business here, as you have to get everything spot on. The club is open to boys and girls aged four to eighteen with the biggest take-up in the four-to-ten group. There is a league system; the Premier League, for the fourteens to eighteens and the distances we travel are huge. There was a game the other day in Dallas and that's nearly nine hours in the coach from here just one way! But we are successful and a number of kids go to sign pro for clubs in Mexico."

So would he come back? "Only if Gareth Southgate offered me a job! Seriously I just enjoy coaching the kids and coming back is the last thing on my mind."

And the health scare? "A couple of years ago I had high blood pressure, the silent killer as my wife calls it. I suffered a small stroke and was out of sorts for three months but I take the medication and all is under control. I want to be around for a while yet."

It was almost time to end the call but first Hammy wanted to sum up his time playing for Boro: "Number one, it was a pleasure to play for Boro. Number two, if I hadn't played for the club, I wouldn't have met my wife, Paula, who is from the town. And number three, my kids love it when we do go back on visits.

"I just couldn't say a bad word about the fans at Boro. It was a superb part of my life. My son still dreams of doing what dad did and playing for the club."

Cheers Gary. Hope the beer chills in the Rio Grande. I'd love to share a bottle, for old time's sake, one day.

6/9/86. Tony Mowbray joins the attack and gets in a good header against Bury. Final Score: 3

30/9/86. Gary Pallister in the thick of it in a night match against Swindon. Final Score 1-0.

10/86. Archie Stephens scores Boro's 3rd goal against Wallsall. Final Score 3-1.

ry Gill scores his first goal for the Club against Carlisle on Boxing Day. Final Score 1-0.

21/2/87. Gary Hamilton scores with a fierce volley against Fulham. Final Score 3-0.

7/3/87.
Alan Kernaghan and David Hodgson threate the Bristol City goal. Final score 1-0.

/87. Lee Turnbull heads a goal for Boro against York City. Final score 3-1.

/87. Bernie Slaven slides in to score against Brentford. Final score 2-0.

6/5/87. Boro fans celebrate the arrival of their heroes.

6/5/87. Rioch and Todd point the way against Wigan. Final score 0-0.

/87. *The players have a welcome bath after promotion has been clinched against Wigan.*

/87. *Stuart Ripley scores Boros 2nd goal against Doncaster Rovers. Final score 2-0.*

Gary Pallister, left and Tony Mowbray

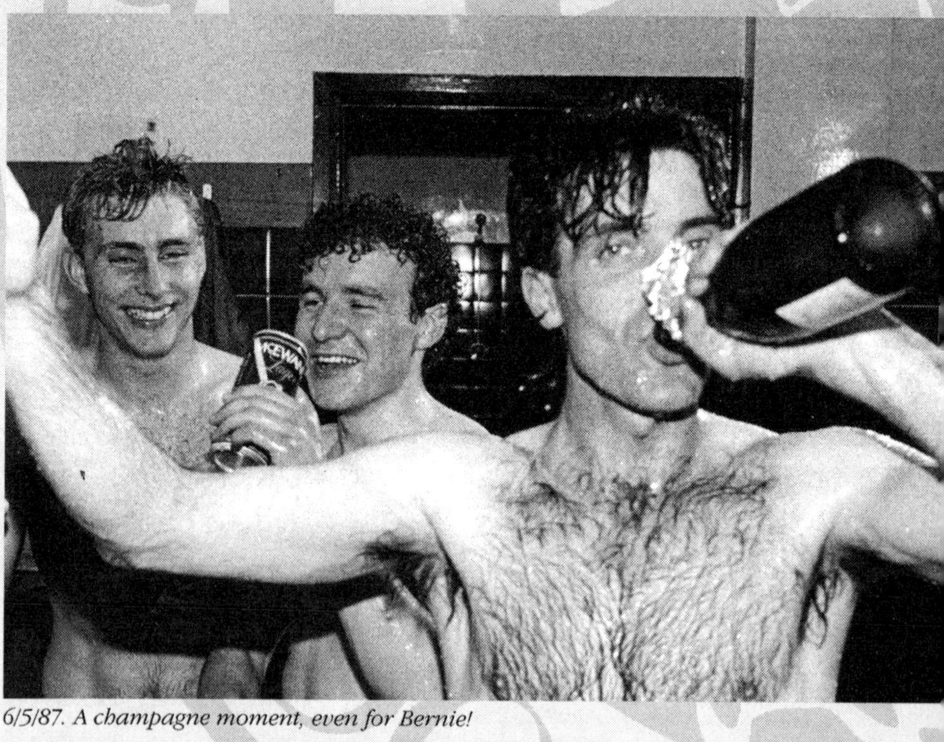

6/5/87. A champagne moment, even for Bernie!

11. Brian Laws: Number 2

Born: Wallsend October 14 1961

From: Huddersfield Town £30,000

Season 1986-87: 35 appearances. 10 goals

Current Occupation: Manager Scunthorpe United Football Club

Providing the managerial merry-go-round doesn't produce another casualty, February 2007 will mark 10 years in the hot seat at Scunthorpe United for Brian Laws. It will also be 20 since, as a young footballer earning a reputation as a goalscoring midfielder, he lay in agony at Ayresome Park after rupturing his knee ligaments, fearing his career was over.

Anniversaries are important and in the footballing life of Brian Laws they are a reminder that throughout his career, triumph and disaster seem never far away. He survived liquidation only to suffer an horrendous injury, then after helping the Boro to the top flight he found himself at the centre of a contract dispute that ended with a move to Nottingham Forest, where he went on to play in five Wembley finals in six years. He was involved in a bust up with Ivano Bonetti at Grimsby that nearly left his managerial career in tatters, now he has survived almost a decade in charge of Scunthorpe.

It would seem that of all the class of '86, Brian Laws has endured more than any on the rollercoaster that is professional football. Despite that, as he welcomes me to Glanford Park, he has changed little since as a young player with time on his hands as he recovered from injury, he joined Gordon Cox and I commentating on the final push to promotion in '87. Lawsy was bright and opinionated as a footballer and commentator and, thankfully, his memory of his time at Ayresome Park was as sharp as ever.

The choice of executive box where we would conduct the interview brought a smile as we settled into the Neil Cox Suite. Neil was one of Bryan Robson's first signings when he took over as manager of the Boro and was the club's first million pound transfer, just nine years after the club came out of liquidation.

Cox also holds the record for Scunthorpe's record transfer fee received after Aston Villa wrote a £350,000 cheque for his services in 1991.

Such a sum paid for a defender would barely make the Sky Sports News headlines today, in the era of a Premiership awash with money. But back in 1986, the thought that Boro would be able to buy a million pound footballer was laughable as the club battled for its very survival. For a footballer with a wife, family and mortgage, they were hard times and the scars are still raw. "All I remember of the summer of 1986 was the sight of the gates of Ayresome Park being locked and, after the liquidator came in, no wages. Remember, we were not the wealthy footballers that are around now. We lived within our means and I must admit that I was scared. I had joined Boro just over a year before. I wasn't enjoying my football at Huddersfield and was glad to get out. I got on straight away with the fans and loved it, but the team were struggling. In my first year under Willie Maddren we just stayed up and then the following season we were relegated. I have to admit, if I had known when I signed what was about to happen financially I wouldn't have put pen to paper."

As the summer dragged on, the financial situation for Laws and many senior players reached breaking point. He recalls: "Archie Stephens and I were getting stressed out and took advice from the PFA. We then went to a Football League tribunal at Oldham and the committee warned Middlesbrough that if they missed one payment of wages then within seven days the players could leave on a free transfer. The tribunal was the last thing the club probably needed, but what were we to do? We had no assurances other than, 'Can you just hang on'. After the tribunal other clubs were alerted to our plight and I spoke to Crystal Palace, but I told them I would wait to see if Boro came through, as I really wanted the club to survive."

Nevertheless, wages clearly had to be met now, otherwise all the work to save the club would be in vain as the playing staff could all walk away. At this moment Steve Gibson came to the rescue. "At that time he was just a young man himself learning his business and he must have been taking a risk getting involved, " remembers Laws. "But he loved the club and all credit to him for what has happened since. I remember Bruce Rioch coming round to my house with a personal cheque signed by Steve Gibson, so he was paying wages just to make sure that we kept the players."

With some of the financial uncertainty removed, training carried on but the build up was hardly ideal. "There we were with odd socks, odd tops, getting changed in cars. It was like a Sunday pub team. We did have our fallouts but credit to Bruce, his coaching then was spot on. He kept discipline and at the same time made training interesting for the players. I have learned as a manager that players can be selfish, thinking only about themselves, but the boss has to worry about everyone and that summer Bruce took on a lot."

The Port Vale game brought a new role for Laws as an attacking midfielder. "We only realised on the Thursday before the opening game that it was going to take place and Bruce told me he wanted me to play in midfield. I couldn't believe it. I was a full-back and said as much but he was determined to get his way, believing that my experience would be better used in midfield to keep things calm and promising it would only be short-term. After every game I was on to Bruce about going back to right-back. But I started hitting some great goals and eventually started to enjoy it.

"The thing I remember about the Port Vale game is the terrific support and on the pitch, the game going at about 100mph. Archie Stephens scored two but we were running on adrenaline and in the last fifteen minutes my legs went. But Bruce continued to work us hard on the training ground and we went on a great run. The manager deserves credit but there were some strong characters in the dressing room who expressed their opinions. Cooper, Mowbray, Pallister, Slaven, Stephens, they could all let you know what they felt and there is nothing worse than hearing from a fellow pro if they think you are not pulling your weight. In the lower leagues you need character, organisation and not be a quiet team. We had all those qualities and more."

As the team pushed on up the table to become clear promotion candidates, the goals flowed from Laws, with eight in 25 league appearances. And then on appearance 26 disaster struck. "We had played a cup-tie against Preston on January 10 and the match should have been postponed, the pitch was frozen. I went up for a header and one of their lads landed on my thigh and I felt an excruciating pain in my knee. I thought it was just twisted and nothing showed up after the game, just a lot of swelling. After a few days the swelling went down and I got through a game against Bury a fortnight later but then, on February 7, the time bomb that was ticking in my knee was about to explode.

"We won a penalty and I placed it on the spot at the Holgate End. I loved to smash penalties and ran up to the ball but as I pulled my leg back it felt like a gun going off – snap! - and in your own body the noise is a hundred times louder. I fell to the floor in agony, and can only remember some of the lads who thought I was lying on the floor after missing, coming over and shouting 'w****r and slaughtering me. I was carried off and they realised it was bad."

It was worse than that. "I thought I had done my cartilage but in fact I had torn my cruciate ligament. In hospital I asked the doctor, if I was I going to play again. That was all I wanted to know and he said: 'I am sorry, I can't tell you that. I just don't know'. I really began to worry and before going in for the operation, I lay in bed with my wife and just said to her, 'I don't know what I am going to do'. No-one seemed to know of a player who had come back from the operation to play at the top again. Then the name of George Burley, the former Ipswich and Sunderland defender, came up. I rang him and after a phone call lasting 90 minutes I felt a bit better, as he had made a recovery from a similar injury. Again credit to Bruce, he asked what I was going to do and when he understood I wanted to stay in the game no matter what. He pushed me into taking my coaching badges.

"The team went on to win promotion while I was doing my rehab and I was delighted for them. But as any player will tell you, if you are not on the field you don't feel fully part of it and it was disappointing to miss out."

Laws won his fight for fitness. "My comeback was in Division Two at Huddersfield on October 10 and I scored after their keeper misplaced a clearance. I belted it and thought, 'This is it, I'm back'."

Ironically it was to be his only goal of the season. Nevertheless he had featured in 17 of the 18 league games since January 1 1988 and his future seemed assured. "Bruce offered me a two-year deal and although we couldn't put pen to paper until the end of the season, went to the press with the news that it was all done and dusted. Sadly, my mum was very ill and passed away before the Chelsea away game in the play-offs and I was allowed some time away from the rest of the squad.

"When I was at home I received a letter offering only a one-year contract. I thought it was an error, a misprint, so I rang Bruce saying I was delighted the lads had gone up but querying the contract I received. He said I had to come to the USA where the team were on tour.

"So after my mum's funeral I set off and I must admit, it was the last place I wanted to be. When I caught up with Bruce he said he had changed his mind and that's the way it was. We got a bit vocal and I said I would never play for him again. I just couldn't believe how you could agree a deal and go back on it.

"I telephoned my wife and she sent a letter to other clubs saying I was available. When I got home I received a phone call from someone saying Brian Clough wanted to speak with me. I thought it was my old teammate Peter Beagrie on the wind-up so I said f**k off and slammed the phone down. It rang again, same thing, Clough accent, and the same reply, 'Stop f**king about' and down went the phone. Anyway, the phone rang again. 'Now young man, I don't take the p*ss, I will ask you this only once, do you want to sign for me at Forest?' It really was Mr Clough. I could only mumble, 'Yes please'. 'Right, well don't f**k about, get down here now'.

"The transfer went to a tribunal but the committee threw out Boro's demand for £250,000 and I signed for Forest for £125,000. I didn't want to move, I am a loyal person, but the contract broke me. I have to say that years later when I was in trouble with my set-to with Ivano Bonetti, a player of mine at Grimsby with whom I had clashed in the dressing room and plates were thrown, the person I rang for advice was Bruce Rioch and he really helped me. Time moves on."

After his playing career ended Brian stayed in the game, and he now puts into practice all he picked up from former bosses as he plays the management game. "Willie Maddren was a nice man, but with the players he was too nice. As a boss you have to make tough decisions and can't be the players' friend. Willie was too caring and some players abused that. Bruce was a strong man but played his football with style, although with some young players was a bit too strong. And as for Mr Clough, well, he was unique."

It was time to go. Brian had to get back to his office, although he did pause to reflect. "Boro are a different club now, all credit again to Steve Gibson. Who would have thought that just ten years after liquidation they would have the Riverside and the Brazilian Player of the Year in Juninho? 1986 was the catalyst though. I think that summer and the season after made me a better person and I always look for Boro's results."

Could he even manage them one day? "Who knows? But I think I have to get Scunthorpe promoted first!"

12. Stuart Ripley: Number 11

Born: Middlesbrough November 20 1967

From: Apprentice

Season 1986-87: 54 appearances, plus two as substitute. Seven goals

Current Occupation: Law and French degree student, University of Central Lancashire, Preston

Wingers often fall into two distinct categories. There are the dribblers, who take the ball to the full-back and, after taunting and teasing their opponent with a trick or step-over, disappear, leaving the defender to face the humiliation of fans and teammates. Then there's the second category, who rely on sheer blistering pace to leave the defender and supporters gasping for air.

The young and talented Mr Ripley of Ayresome Park falls, with absolute certainty, into the second category.

Boro fans who remember '86 can close their eyes and see a tall, powerful, blonde-haired winger running towards the Holgate End, tempting the full-back to come towards him and then pushing the ball into the green space behind the defender. Suddenly, with a terrific burst of acceleration, he is clear, charging towards the fans and then crossing, where Archie Stephens rises to send a header crashing past a helpless goalkeeper.

Sadly, the script didn't always have a happy ending, and as my car pulled up outside Stuart's executive home in a leafy estate outside Blackburn I can also see Stephens and Slaven looking accusingly at the young winger as a mis-hit cross zipped into the crowd. But back then Stuart was only 18, a diamond who needed polishing. But most important to the fans, he was a Boro lad living out their dream.

"Stuart, Stuart Ripley, Stuart Ripley on the wing" was the chant from the fans and at first it took some getting used to for the Acklam lad. " I used to stand in the Holgate End or the Boys End as a kid," he reflects. "My heroes were David Mills and, when I was younger, John Hickton. And now here I was on the pitch. It was incredible. At school I never really thought about being a professional footballer. My mam and dad were both schoolteachers and naturally stressed the importance of getting a good education. They were probably a bit scared that if I put everything into football I might have nothing to fall back on."

So football continued to be part, but not the only part, of Stuart's schooldays at Whinney Banks, then known as Oaklands School. "Back then, I just loved playing. These days, with all the financial rewards, some kids think about a career in the game for all the wrong reasons, but I just enjoyed every game from a kickabout with my pals to playing for the town team, Boro Boys. We had a good side and won the England Schools Trophy. I actually played central midfield then and winning the cup brought scouts to the games. I suppose at about 15 I started to think I could make it and John Jennings, a scout from Boro, got me to go down to Ayresome Park and I signed schoolboy forms while Malcolm Allison was manager and then apprentice forms under Willie Maddren."

The education-football debate was, thankfully, resolved in the Ripley household. "I had a long talk to mam and dad. I said I could always go back to education but you get few chances to play football for a career and if I didn't give this opportunity everything, I might regret it for the rest of my life. I did promise my parents that if it didn't work out I would go back to my education. I kept my word, as 20 years on I am doing a degree course!"

The problem was that no matter how determined Stuart may have been, Boro were facing a financial crisis that could shatter the dream. "I was just a teenager living at home so I didn't have financial worries, but I didn't have a track record in the game either. If the club had folded then the senior players could have moved on. But what were Gary Parkinson, Lee Turnbull and I going to do? We were just boys whose careers hadn't started. I really think that we were the most vulnerable to going out of the game."

In common with all the class of '86, Stuart has his own opinion of the manager, Bruce Rioch. "The previous season I had played on loan for a few games at Bolton and might have gone there permanently, but Bruce stopped all that talk. He came to watch me play and just said I was going to be part of his plans at Boro and that was that.

"In my opinion he was the best thing that happened to Boro. Okay, some would say he was direct, aggressive and confrontational, but that was exactly what was needed. He put in place a simple but effective pattern of play and bullied a young bunch of inexperienced lads into a good football side playing 4-4-2, passing, not thumping, the ball forward, and this was in a division where some sides were simply out to give a bunch of kids a good kicking. I look back on that season and the one after, when we went up again, and I can say that even though I played in a Premiership-winning side at Blackburn, the football we played then was probably the best I was ever privileged to play."

There were, of course, confrontations. "As a young kid I had sensitive skin and hated shaving, and I was fined for coming unshaven to training and Bruce could scare you stiff. Nowadays players are on so much money, what is a manager going to do? If he puts them in the reserves they will still pick up their money. But back then we were on pennies in comparison and if Bruce said he would let you rot in the reserves for the rest of your life, you were terrified that he might just do it!"

After playing against Port Vale, the first game back at Ayresome was a League Cup tie against Hartlepool on September 2 1986 in front of a crowd of 7,735. As Boro attacked the East End, the first goal since the financial crisis padlocked the gates was scored. "I can still see it now," says Ripley, smiling. "It came from a throw and as the ball came to me, it bounced once and I curled it into the far corner of the net. It was also my first goal for the Boro and it was a terrific feeling."

Being a local lad didn't mean the crowd gave you an easy time. "I was a winger playing in front of the 'chicken run' (the old terracing area of the South Stand at Ayresome Park) and was in the line of fire. Unless you were doing your best they let you have it! They wouldn't accept non-triers for a second and it made you grow up. Remember, until then, in schoolboys' teams, all everyone said was you were the best thing since sliced bread. Now you were in front of all these blokes shouting you were crap if you misplaced a cross. It was an experience."

Nevertheless, Ayresome Park in '86 was an intimidating place for the opposition. "I have spoken to players over the years and they would say, 'We hated going to Ayresome Park'. The atmosphere for us was terrific. As the fans banged the wooden boards and then there was all that foot stamping, you would look at the other team and think, 'They don't fancy this one bit'. It would give us almost a goal start.

"I remember one game against Bournemouth. They were top of the league and on a grey November afternoon we hammered them 4-0. I got a goal and it all just clicked. The crowd was about 11,000 but it seemed about ten times that with all the noise. We were really up for it and jumped above them into top spot. There was also the Wigan game when we went up. The crowd came onto the pitch and I was a bit frightened as they grabbed shirts, shorts and God knows what else! But what a night, as we celebrated going up."

It was a team on and off the pitch. "Yes I did go to the Madison every now and then. The place was buzzing for the three years after liquidation. The club and the town were on the up and if the team does well, so does the whole area. Bruce liked the lads to go to social events and meet the fans. It's strange, but it changed a couple of seasons later when Bruce signed Peter Davenport. He was a great lad and a good player, but for some reason that signing rocked the boat and affected the relationships within the team."

Inevitably, comparisons are made between Stuart Ripley and another Boro lad making his mark. "Stewart Downing looks similar to the way I played but the quality of delivery he puts into the box is the difference. I would like to think I achieved that later in my career, but at the same age I didn't have that."

After leaving Boro and winning a title at Blackburn, his career came to an end at Southampton. "I don't miss football but I do miss training," he says surprisingly. "It got to a stage where the match at the end of the week was unbearable. I had injuries and just didn't enjoy it. I could have played on but I would have been playing purely for money.

"I am a degree student now and we do chat about football in the classroom. There is a novelty value when I say I used to play, but after a while you are just another student. They really don't know about my career and in football you are soon forgotten as the new kids come on the scene. I still go back to Middlesbrough to see my family, I have no plans to move back as one day, when the degree is finished and the kids are grown, I would like to live abroad. But wherever I go, I will still be a Boro fan.

"It was a unique part of my life and unique in the life of Middlesbrough FC, but I hope that the club never finds itself in that situation again financially. It did produce, though, some great times and in terms of sheer enjoyment, to go from the terraces to pulling on the red shirt to enjoying the buzz of promotion, even though I have a championship medal, it was the happiest time of my career."

Stuart, Stuart Ripley, Stuart Ripley on the wing...

13. Bernie Slaven: Number 7

Born: Paisley November 13 1960

From: Albion Rovers £25,000

Season 1986-87: 58 appearances 21 goals

Current Occupation: Century fm - Three Legends and Boro match commentary

On the way to meeting up with Bernie, I took a drive along Westbourne Road in Middlesbrough. Then, as in 1986, a tidy row of terraced houses stands within walking distance of what was once Ayresome Park.

At a cost of £25,000, number 27 was Bernie's first home on Teesside and on £300 a week, the one hundred per cent mortgage dug deep into the Slaven family's monthly budget. But he was scoring goals and popular with the fans, who sometimes on a Friday evening on the way home from The Linthorpe or The Cambridge pubs would stand outside and shout, "There's only one Bernie Slaven" as he tried to get some sleep ahead of matchday.

However, sleep was to be in short supply in the summer of '86 as the club went into liquidation and his payment to the building society bounced.

Twenty years on and Bernie's profile has never been higher. An opinionated member of the Three Legends phone-in on Century fm, his determination to tell it as he sees it occasionally brings him into conflict with the Boro. Terry Venables had him removed from the match programme and Steve McClaren was hardly a fan of the phone-in. Some current players also find his views unacceptable and last season Mark Schwarzer even volleyed footballs towards the press box in Bernie's direction.

On the pitch Bernie was a deadly striker. Long after his career is over, his opinions divide as often as a linesman's flag would be raised against Boro's number 7. But beyond the media image he is, a hugely generous character. After all, he gave away the entire proceeds of his autobiography *Legend?* to the Ann Charlton Lodge for MS sufferers in Redcar, a sum of more than £32,000, because he visits Boro fans who are residents there.

Inside Bernie, the intense goalscoring desire that brought 147 goals for Boro still burns intensely. A week before I caught up with him he had played in a charity game in aid of Motor Neurone Disease Charities at Marske, scored twice and had a blazing row with his teammates as the side fell to a 4-2 defeat against a team from TV soap Emmerdale. Everyone else was delighted with a 2,000 crowd and a big sum raised for charity, but not Bernie. "My teams don't lose to a bunch of soap stars," was the verdict. The swollen knee and limp as he opened the gate to let me in were reminders that on the pitch, he still plays for real.

Bernie lives just outside Thirsk, happy to be in the countryside and today he was in a particularly good mood, as his dad was visiting from Glasgow. The father-son relationship is a strong one. It was "Da" who nurtured his love of the game as they watched Celtic together, taught him how to play, made sure that he kept on trying for a professional career when all looked lost and insisted in 1986, when Boro seemed to be going out of existence, that he stayed at Ayresome Park.

"Clubs like Middlesbrough survive Bernard, they always do," were his words, before he sent his son an envelope containing the cash to pay his monthly mortgage.

They do fall out. Bernie was annoyed that the subject of his penalty miss in the recent Masters tournament was brought up. "Did you see him, Ali?" asked Slaven senior. "I told him when he was seven, most keepers dive to the right and does he listen? No! His penalty was rubbish!"

Da then set off after the Irish setter which was in pursuit of some workmen close to the three cars that were parked in the drive.

Back in 1986 Bernie didn't have a car. "I walked from Westbourne Road to Ayresome Park and one of the lads would give me a lift to wherever we were training. The club was bust and we used to train at Stewart Park, Hall Drive, but more often Longlands College, then Bruce would shout, 'Leave the cars here and jog to training'! It kept you fit."

Bernie is in no doubt that Bruce Rioch was the man responsible for keeping the players together. "He was just what we needed. He was regimental but don't forget we had been relegated the season before and some needed a good kick up the backside. Despite all the worries he kept us together, saying 'Look, none of us are getting paid, including me. But let's train as normal, enjoy it and do the town proud'. Without Bruce half the lads would have just sat all summer in front of the TV.

"Training was intense. He once sent Pally home saying he was going through the motions and that if he didn't want to do it to f*** off. Pally had just jogged to Longlands and now he was walking back to Ayresome in the pouring rain like a naughty schoolkid! Bruce also liked the contact side of the game and shouted numbers out in the gym to go one-on-one. He always seemed to shout out Lawsy's number and kick him in the air..."

As the crisis deepened, Bernie joined the rest of the lads picking up his money from the town hall as the consortium and later the PFA paid their basic wage. Some, like Peter Beagrie and Don O'Riordan, left. "I did think at the time they were jumping ship. The lads were all in it together but looking back, who knows? They must have had their reasons but I can honestly say I never thought of quitting."

Despite the club's perilous state up to the start of the season, the players prepared for the Port Vale opening game as normally as possible. "We didn't get involved with any members of the consortium. That was up to Bruce and we were in a way cocooned in our environment. Even so when I watched the news the Friday before the match and it was announced we were saved, it was a huge relief."

Memories of the match at the Victoria Ground, Hartlepool, are still fresh. "We got on the team bus to go to Hartlepool dressed in some scruffy gear. Pally had the worst jumper I had ever seen on. I think that all the pressure of the summer told in the end and we threw away a two-goal lead to just get a point. The size of the crowd disappointed me. I thought, 'Bloody hell, I have spent all summer struggling to get by and only just over 3,000 could be bothered to turn up!'. I thought it would be full, but when we got back to Ayresome and the Holgate got in full cry there was no better place to play. The Holgate End was great. All working class lads, with a smell of bovril, fags and pee."

The Stephens-Slaven partnership terrorised defences, scoring 33 league goals between them. "Archie was a great foil for me. He smoked I didn't. He drank, I didn't. But on the field we complemented each other. He was a tough guy, great in the air and I fed off him. Archie was ideal for me."

The strikers needed, however, service. "Stuart Ripley had great pace and he used it to great effect. He wasn't a dribbler, he used to go up to the full-back and then knock the ball to one side, hit it thirty yards and tear after it. Mind you, his crossing could be a bit dodgy. Archie and I once said we would have more chance of getting on a cross if we stood in the Holgate!"

As the season went on, so the belief grew. "I remember one game at Newport, a horrible wet afternoon and Tony Mowbray flinging himself at the ball to score a last minute winner. We just had this belief. Before a game at Ayresome, Coops, Ripper and Mogga would be banging on the glass door getting everyone wound up and Bruce went around giving out last minute encouragement. Parky always needed a bit of an arm around the shoulder, the Power Game would blast out from the PA.

Hardly U2, but it did the trick and out we went to get another three points."

Chatting to Bernie, like all the players, you get the feeling that their captain of '86 will be their captain forever: "Mowbray – Mogga - was my great skipper. When he led the team out you felt invincible. He wasn't a shouter, it was his presence on the pitch. As a local lad, you knew how much Middlesbrough meant to him."

The promotion clincher at home to Wigan was unforgettable. "I thought Archie had scored in the second half with a header but it was ruled out. Then, just before the end, the ref said, 'Right lads, next time the ball is near the tunnel that's it'. And off we went. The dressing room atmosphere was superb and I can remember going up to the directors' box and standing on the edge celebrating with the fans. The only downside was someone handed me a can of lager and I cut my hand on the ring pull. Good job I don't drink!"

It didn't end there for Bernie. "The next three years were the best of my career. I helped the team to the top flight, played international football and got Boro to Wembley. It was all down to the spirit of '86."

After seven and a half great years he left Boro for Port Vale, Darlington and then after his career finished set up soccer schools, before the media knocked on his door. "I love working on radio but thinking back to '86 Parky's dad used to tape some clowns called Brownlee and Cox doing commentary. Parky used to wind me up by saying they had said I'd hit the cameraman when I knew the shot was just wide. If someone had said then that I would do their job one day, I would have laughed."

The spirit of '86 is still there. "I still see Parky, who hasn't changed. He is still the same as the young lad from Thornaby who I first met, and I catch up with Gilly, Pearsy and Pally regularly."

And for the future? "Not a clue. I hope to work in radio for many years but my values are rooted in that dressing room 20 years ago. Work hard and don't forget that in life, anything worth doing is never achieved the easy way."

Bruce Rioch once described Bernie to new signing Paul Kerr as like a hippie on the motorway of life. He was probably spot on. But there are a few miles left yet in the wolfman of '86.

14. Archie Stephens: Number 8

Born: Liverpool May 19 1954

From: Bristol Rovers £20,000

Season 1986-87: 57 appearances 18 goals

Current Occupation: Electrician's mate

As Manchester United stormed to a Premiership title in the early 1990s, TV pundit Alan Hansen was ridiculed for a remark he made early in the season claiming United wouldn't win anything relying only on kids. The kids, clearly, proved him wrong but it was hard not to feel a bit of sympathy for Hansen. After all, most teams rely on a blend of youth and experience to bring success. The Boro babes of 1986 were certainly grateful for an old fashioned centre forward with razor sharp elbows, who helped them in the school of hard knocks that was Division Three.

When Archie Stephens was on the pitch opposition defenders and their goalkeeper rarely had a quiet afternoon.

Professional football came late to Arthur, as he was christened. It wasn't until the age of 27 that he made his debut for Bristol Rovers, then managed by the former Boro and Leeds full-back Terry Cooper, after Archie's non-league side Melksham Town pocketed a £3,000 transfer fee. In March 1985 he signed on the pitch at Ayresome Park at half-time in a home game against Sheffield United as Willie Maddren looked to the striker to help keep Boro in Division Two, taking a gamble at £20,000.

Archie settled into his new club, and after initially renting, bought a house in Great Ayton that still remains home. In the current football climate where players are paid exorbitant wages, drive expensive cars and often live far from their fan base Archie is a throwback to how the game used to be. He played hard and after 90 minutes enjoyed a pint and a cigarette with the supporters.

Some things never change. As we began to look back on his part in '86, he reminded me that interviews were thirsty work and I would have to treat him to a pint in the workingmens' club afterwards. "No problem," was the reply, No one argues with Archie, even now!

Although Willie Maddren signed Archie, within a year Bruce Rioch was in charge and soon manager and player were on a collision course. "At first Bruce and I didn't get on," he admits. "He thought I was a typical scouse scallywag and favoured Dave Currie as his striker. At the end of one training session at Ayresome Park he sent Gary Hamilton and me off to do some sprints, as we weren't involved in the first team for the next game. Anyway, we finished and had a shower and I was all set to go when Hammy said we couldn't leave as Bruce was having a meeting in the TV room next to the dressing room with the rest of the lads.

"I said, 'f*** him, I'm going home', but Hammy pleaded with me to at least see Bruce. So I tapped on the door, opened it, and said, 'Excuse me Bruce'. He looked up and just exploded. 'What do you want and what are you doing not shaving?' Remember, I am a thirty-two-year-old bloke, not a fresh-faced kid. So I said, 'Look, I am not involved with the first team and want to go home'. Bruce just launched into, 'Get out and shut the door'. Well I shut it all right and nearly took it off its hinges and the gaffer just said to the stunned players, 'He is going nowhere'. Mind you, he was right!

After a shaky start the pair forged a relationship. "He was a bit of a dictator to the younger players but not to the likes of Stephen Pears, Brian Laws and I, we just said what we thought. Bruce knew I liked a drink and a smoke but just let me get on with it as long as I was scoring the goals."

The summer of 1986 was difficult for everyone. "It hit home to me what liquidation meant when staff from the Blue Bell Garage in Acklam came to the ground while we were training to take back their sponsored cars. About five of the lads had cars and when training was over, the cars had all gone. The only thing of mine left was the kid's baby seat, lying in Warwick Street!"

As the financial crisis deepened and with no wages coming in, Archie and Brian Laws went to a Football League tribunal to try to get released from their contracts. The players lost the appeal: "I didn't want to leave but I had a wife and kids to feed and a mortgage to pay. Some said we were being greedy trying to get away but I didn't see it that way and I know other players had clubs waiting if the worst had happened. It was only sensible to try to protect your future. Later that summer I had a call from Terry Cooper, who had signed me for Rovers and was now at Bristol City, saying he would take me if the club went under. Thankfully Boro survived.

"At the end of the season after the final game at Doncaster, Bruce asked me to sit alongside him on the bus on the way back. He said: 'Well done, great season I'm glad I kept you, but if you had got a good solicitor for that tribunal you would have got a free!' I had no complaints. I had never wanted to go and it was the best season of my career."

Archie made an instant impact in the opening game against Port Vale: "We got changed in the Portakabins at Hartlepool and all the lads were up for it. My first goal was a trademark header but the second was special. I remember Hammy going through and shouting, 'push it!', but the ball just sat up and I hit this left-foot volley right on the sweet spot. The keeper was off his line and from 30 yards out it just sailed in...get in there! And that was the beginning."

The partnership of Slaven and Stephens was prolific and between them they scored 33 league goals. "Bernie and I clicked. I used to do the hustle and bustle, mixing it with the defenders, and Bernie would pick up the pieces. I wasn't bothered who scored but it certainly worked alright. We were great on the pitch but didn't mix socially, he had Pally for that!"

It was a season filled with great goals but Archie's favourite was reserved for an away day at Blackpool on March 21 1987. But the trip to Bloomfield Road got off to a strange start: "When we checked in to the hotel on the Friday night, Colin Todd said, 'Are you going for a pint tonight?' I couldn't believe it. It was always the same for me, no drinking after Wednesday until the game was finished and I said as much to Toddy who replied, 'Well there's a boozer round the corner if you fancy one'.

"I think he was just testing me out, but when I got back to the room Paul Kerr said, 'If Toddy is okay for us to have a pint let's have one', so we ordered room service, a lager, bitter and a whisky. We had three pints and that was it. The following morning I went to pay at reception. Up popped Bruce. 'Had a good night Archie? Have you had a drink?', 'No boss' I replied. 'You're lying Archie, I have your room bill and who had the whisky?' I just blamed Paul and legged it!"

Bruce was good to me that trip. He overlooked the pints and agreed that if I did well, I could have Monday off and stay with the family in Liverpool. I scored the only goal as Parky crossed and I dived full-length to score with a header from the edge of the box. Five thousand Boro fans went wild behind the goal. It was a special moment.

As the season drew to a close promotion edged nearer. "The Wigan game was the clincher and we did everything but score. I had a great chance, Stuart Ripley put the cross in and nine times out of ten I would have scored. I headed it down under the keeper but it spun back into his arms. At the end, though, it didn't matter and we were up. It was the first time in my professional career that I had been promoted. We should have been champions as well, but we dropped some silly points and Bournemouth nicked it. We'd hammered them 4-0 at Ayresome as well."

The season after it was all over for Archie at Boro. "Bruce said he was letting me go to Carlisle. I didn't agree, I thought I was still fit enough to do a job, but he was adamant, saying he was giving youth a chance. I thought he might have gone for buying someone like Ian Baird to replace me and asked who was getting my shirt. Bruce thought different. His choice was Alan Kernaghan. Kernaghan! F*** me, he couldn't lace my boots! But it was his choice and that was it."

From Carlisle next destination was Darlington, where he helped the Quakers to promotion from the Conference before the full-time whistle blew on his career: "I worked as a crane driver for four years, then a bit of ducking and diving and for the last seven years have worked as an electrician's mate on sites at ICI and other chemical plants. I did take my prelim badge but probably needed a kick up the a**e if I was to stay in the game. I have no regrets. I wouldn't survive these days, even back when I was playing the refs would say, 'Archie, keep the elbows down'. And then 'Whack!' The defender would catch you from behind. I would just wait and get them back. I loved the physical side of the game, but it's gone now."

So too, of course, is Ayresome Park. "I loved it. Coming from Eastville, Bristol Rovers' ground, which was surrounded by a dog track and was a bit of a tip, Ayresome was great and when the crowds came back it had a terrific atmosphere. The Riverside is fantastic but it's not the same as the Holgate. I wouldn't have swapped that season in '86. It was my best ever as a pro and a good way, as it turned out, to finish at the Boro."

We had talked for a good hour. The memories were still fresh but Archie was ready for that pint...

15. Lee Turnbull: Number 12

Born: Stockton September 27 1967

From: Apprentice September 1985

Season 1986-87: Appearances 16, nine as substitute. Five Goals

Current Occupation: Community Manager Scunthorpe United FC

Steel is as crucial to the history and economy of Scunthorpe as it is to Teesside. It seems appropriate, therefore, that a son of our steel river is now spreading the football message to youngsters who dream one day of playing for the Lincolnshire club.

Lee Turnbull lived out his dream as he moved on from the terraces of Ayresome Park to playing for his beloved Boro. Today he remains a devoted fan.

As we enjoyed a cup of coffee, before looking back on '86, Lee was pleased to have been invited to the Riverside to watch the Boro defeat Chelsea. He was out of his seat yelling with the rest of the supporters as Mark Viduka struck a late winner to send the champions back to London defeated.

The only cloud on the Turnbull horizon was that his son had asked for the latest Arsenal strip and not Boro's. But you sensed that dad would be using all his powers of persuasion to ensure that Turnbull junior had a change of heart.

After poring over the old programmes I had brought along that afternoon in Scunthorpe, Lee remembered his journey from fan to Boro striker. "I used to follow the team home and away. For big games at Ayresome I would get the bus with my schoolmates from Stockton and be in the queue for the Holgate from 12.30pm. Our heroes were Heine Otto and Bosco Jankovic, and anyone really who played in the red shirt. I went to Swansea to watch the team in an FA Cup tie, suffered heartbreak as we lost to Wolves in the quarter-final, and at West Brom I had my scarf pinched and was chased down the street by Albion fans. Just the usual stuff following the Boro!

"There was one match in February 1983 which I remember well. We went to Oldham on a miserable afternoon. Most of the other games that day were called off and yet there we were in our donkey jackets, soaked to the skin, watching Boro get beat 3-0. I wouldn't have been anywhere else. This was my team."

As a young striker, Lee's career got off to an intimidating start. "Willie Maddren gave me my debut in a Full Members Cup tie at Hull on November 5 1985. Early on I broke Richard Jobson's nose when I went for a flick-on and caught him. Hull had some big guys playing that night, including Billy Whitehurst, and they were threatening to give me a good kicking. I was only 18 and decided to go on the left-wing to get out of their way!"

After Bruce Rioch took over he gave the teenager a chance to help the club stay up. "I came on as sub for Colin Cooper in the final home game against Millwall and really enjoyed it. The 3-0 win gave us a chance of avoiding the drop. Before the final game at Shrewsbury we stayed at Lilleshall and Bruce said I would be in from the start. It was a disaster, I didn't play well and got distracted by trouble in the crowd as coppers' helmets were flying on pitch. I was trying to see where my family were in the stand to make sure they were okay. It was all too much and after we were relegated I sat in the dressing room in tears."

As it did for the majority of his team mates, the summer brought its financial problems. "I was still at home with mam and dad so it wasn't too bad, Mam just went without the £20 a week I used to give her. After a while we went to the town hall for our wages. Gary Rowell used to pick me up to save my bus fare and after training on a Friday we would sit with the binmen and other council workers waiting for wages. A hatch would then open up and we would receive brown envelopes with our money. Mine was as thin as an After Eight mint wrapper. But I never thought about leaving. Grimsby and Sheffield United were interested but I just said no thanks, not interested."

The Rioch factor was starting to work on the squad. "Bruce kept us together, he ruled by fear and the lads nicknamed him Gadaffi after the Libyan dictator. But he had to instill resilience and discipline in some raggy young lads and a pit yakker like Coops! He was a headmaster figure but just what was needed. I didn't have too many run-ins with him. He would give me bollockings, of course, but I remember one occasion when I went to his office as Archie Stephens was having a barren spell and I thought I should be in the team. 'Any chance of a game Bruce?' I asked. The reply? 'F**k off and shut the door on the way out'. I didn't ask again."

The historic match against Port Vale brought a place on the bench. "We were really up for it but the late kick-off worked against us. We were all sitting watching the results coming in, desperate to play, wanting to get the game on. So come kick-off we tore into them and went two up but we ran out of steam. If we had started at three o'clock I am certain we would have won 4-0."

After the opening day draw the next league game was at Wigan and because of an injury to Archie, Lee was in from the start. "August 30th is my Mam's birthday so it was a special day to start with, but at first things didn't look good. In fact they battered us in the first half at Springfield Park on a hot afternoon. But in the second came a moment I will always remember. Bernie ran from the halfway line to the edge of the box and slipped the ball to me on my left-hand side. That wasn't my strongest side but as I let it roll across I thought just hit it, and in front of the Boro fans the ball flew into the net. I didn't know where to run or what to do and for a few seconds I froze. I then ran one way only to have to turn around and run in the opposite direction when I remembered where my mates were in the crowd. Great feeling but I was numb for about 15 minutes."

Despite the delight at scoring in a 2-0 win, it was back to the bench and reserve team duty. "I can't complain, Archie Stephens and Bernie Slaven were a great partnership and were, naturally the first choice. Archie was great, though. In training always saying, 'Lee get your wings up when you jump,' meaning get the elbows into the defenders. Bernie had great control and an eye for goal and I just tried to learn off them. They used to go and watch the home reserve games, a lot of the first team did. Tony Mowbray was my hero and a great captain. I used to feel ten feet tall if, after scoring in a reserve match, he would pull me to one side the following day to say, 'well done'."

Towards the end of the season Lee featured in the final eight games, making six starts and scoring three goals: "Against York I finished one off at the Holgate End and that was something I always wanted to do since being a kid. In the next home game I smashed in a 25-yard shot against Brentford and when Gillingham came to Ayresome for a big promotion match I scored with a header in a 3-0 win. The scorers that night Stephens, Slaven and Turnbull - what a strikeforce!

"Then there was the Wigan promotion night. I should have scored. Gary Hamilton crossed and I should have hit it with my left foot, but chose to go with the right and put it wide. There was a picture of it the following night in the Gazette and I still couldn't believe I had missed! We went up, though, and when all the fans came on I was tempted to stay on the field as I saw my friends in the crowd, but I went down the tunnel with Gary Parkinson. Parky is my big mate. We played for Stockton West End together as kids, we were pals from the age of ten and also played for the town and county sides and went on trials together. We were as thick as thieves, so it was good to be celebrating promotion together. Mind you, Bruce wouldn't let us celebrate until it was confirmed that Swindon had only drawn and we were actually up. Even at that stage Bruce was being meticulous, checking all the facts.

"In the dressing room it was chaos, all dancing and going wild. I still have a bronze-framed copy of the Gazette photo of Gary and I hugging each other."

The party continued. "After we went in the directors' box to wave at the fans we were invited with our girlfriends to the boardroom, where a buffet was laid on, and I can say that most of the lads had a fair few drinks. A suggestion was made that we go to the Madison and then someone said, 'No chance, we have a match on Saturday and Bruce will find out'!"

The final game was at Doncaster. "Again I missed a chance and slid into our fans.

We were delighted to go up but a bit upset not to be champions, as Bournemouth pipped us to top spot. After the game Coops was stripped naked by the fans, but I remember in the dressing room afterwards a kid crying his eyes out as he had nearly been crushed in the crowd. I felt sorry for him and gave him my shirt. Years later I got a letter from him saying he still had the away shirt and he was proud to have it. The home shirt for that season I kept and dad looks after it for me."

Sadly, Lee would never pull on a Boro shirt again, as he was transferred early the following season. "It was all a bit of a rush. I was with the squad as we lost at Sunderland in the League Cup. When we got back to Ayresome Park after the game, Bruce said, 'Graham Taylor at Aston Villa wants you, I suggest you go'. I was stunned. The following day I drove down and the deal was done, with Kevin Poole and £50,000 going the other way. I agreed a three-year deal, but I was in a daze and felt disillusioned and rejected."

The Villa experience was short. "I wanted to play and wasn't prepared to be patient. Steve Harrison tried to help, as did Graham Taylor, but I was determined to play so I left after six months to go to Doncaster. In truth I think I realised that the bottom two divisions were my level. I ended up in central midfield as I played for Chesterfield, back to Doncaster then a spell at Wycombe under Martin O'Neill before Scunthorpe, where I had four knee operations in 18 months and then my final move to Darlington, where I hung my boots up at 31 after a back injury."

Lee's passion for football endures. "I did my coaching badges and was involved with non-league teams Barrow and Southport before I began doing match reports on the opposition for Brian Laws here at Scunthorpe and, of course, my role as community officer for the club."

Lee took a final look at my photo of the squad of '86. "I know I am greyer and heavier now but it seems like yesterday, Mam kicking me out of bed, meeting up with Pally and Parky, travelling to Ayresome. It was like a big boys' club.

"I truly lived the dream. I might have only made 19 appearances, but no one can take it away. I am proud that as a Boro fan I made it to play and score for the club. And I still have that shirt."

16. Memories of the fans

We asked Boro fans to offer their recollections of the summer of '86. Here's what they had to say...

I was closer to what was going on than many Boro fans during the summer of '86. I was working for the Council in the Municipal Buildings in Middlesbrough. I ran errands all summer so that I could listen at the door to the committee rooms where the consortium held their press conferences. I hung on every word although it was sometimes difficult to decipher what was being said, beyond the door. It was agonising not knowing whether the club would survive and there were a lot of pre-occupied folk around, such as Steve Gibson and Colin Henderson as well as the Council's top legal officials.

I recall various deadlines passing, but, Friday August 22 was D-Day. A press conference had been called for teatime. The whole office was buzzing that day with speculation as to whether the club could be saved. I worked late and went over to see what was happening. There was a real nervous tension in the air. The door was shut at first, but, as the press conference began it had to be opened, such was the interest.

The announcement that the Football League had accepted the consortium offer to creditors and that Middlesbrough would kick off the season the following day against Port Vale at Hartlepool provided such a feeling of relief. Relief turned to reality the following evening, when I saw Archie Stephens score two cracking goals in that infamous first ever match for born again Boro.

Simon Dale

****

The summer of 86 was a vital one in my life in two ways really. Firstly, I was doing my A levels. Secondly, and more importantly, the Boro were in serious danger of going out of existence and whether or not I passed my A levels began to take on something of an irrelevance. Qualifications and a career I may have needed but I could get around the lack of A levels if that's how it turned out (or so I thought as a naive teenager). Getting over the lack of Middlesbrough FC in my life was a different matter. Thankfully I passed the exams and just a week later, the news that my beloved Boro had been saved made it a good end to a worrying time. It also meant that the majority of my student grant from my subsequent admission to university went on following the Boro - no wonder I never did get that degree!!

Simon Bolton, Redcar

****

You could fill the Riverside three times over with all the people who say they were at Hartlepool for Boro v Port Vale in 1986. But I really was there, and I remember it vividly. After the gloom of locked gates and training sessions in the park there came hope. When it looked as though Archie Stephens was going to shoot from an improbable distance, I shouted out for him to pass instead. But he shot, and what a goal. I remember just as vividly that we should have had a throw-in before their second goal but the linesman missed it. It still rankles.

Before that great day, I'd sent some money - I think it was the pathetic sum of £25 - to the Save the Boro fund. After we were saved, Steve Gibson sent it back. Once a hero, always a hero.

I was 19 in 86, about the same age as the most of the players. Someone at school had once played against Stuart Ripley (and got skinned). There was a great sense of excitement, of fighting against the odds - with the nothing-to-lose unknown youngsters, local lads, all blonde flicks and fresh faces, combined with the experience of Archie, Bernie and Stephen Pears and making a potent combination. Offside or not, selfish or not, it was always Bernie who was first for me. Happy days, and none more so than on the pitch at Ayresome after promotion a few months later. Boro were back.

Mark Davies

****

I am 49 and had been going to Ayresome Park since my dad took me as lad of 11 in 1968 - so 18 years later in 1986 I was still going regular through the Charlton era and into lesser dizzy heights through Murdoch, Neal, Allison and Maddren, 1986 was when the club literally bottomed out. There was no way we were going to survive and play in the 1986/7 season. Players were leaving and "owners" leaving a sinking ship. Each day I read Ray Robertson's column in The Northern Echo for snippets of information. Eventually Steve Gibson pulled the rabbit out of the hat and we haven't look back. I can remember standing level with the 18-yard line in the terrace at the Victoria Ground - Hartlepool had let us use their ground for the first game against Port Vale - and feeling the buzz of the hardcore Boro support that day. It was a carnival atmosphere with an overwhelming feeling of pride that we had survived. To put icing on the day Archie Stephens cracked a speculative half volley into the goal we were level with. The result unimportant - the presence of Middlesbrough Football Club 1986 in Football League Division 3 much more significant.

Brian Worth

****

I was just about to turn 18, and like most in the area unemployed, but something was buzzing around town, the football team, most looking like me, someone you could relate to, bleached blonde wedges haircuts!!!!

But my one abiding memory is Archie Stephen's thunderbolt v Port Vale that Saturday evening at Hartlepool. Pick that one out then son!!!! 2-2, that'll do for starters. I just remember that season was one colossal battle with Bournemouth. And one great mystery, did Gary Gill ever get a hair out of place???!!!

Ian Stephens

****

I remember being nine years old, I'd just finished my stint as World Cup 86 monitor for the class. I still remember walking down Redcar High Street with my mam and seeing all the posters begging to 'Save the Boro'. As a nine-year-old I didn't really understand but I was still determined to follow the Boro forever. My classmates all agreed with me and we used to have competitions to remember the starting line up. Pears, Laws, Cooper, Mowbray, Parkinson, Pallister, Slaven, Stephens, Hamilton, Gill, Ripley. Still in my mind today. Archie was my favourite along with Bernie. My mates used to call me the Wolfman because I had longish hair like him. I loved it being likened to my hero. I was always him down the park with my number seven shirt on. I used to go to the Reserve games in the hope of meeting the first teamers. I still remember the first game against Port Vale at the Victoria Ground. Great days though as a naive nine year old I obviously didn't understand the severity of the situation. The class of 86 along with Sir Bruce will always hold a special part in my memory.

Wayne Chalmers

****

I remember in 1986 at Ayresome Junior School in the assembly hall we had a poster of Gary Pallister on the wall. My dad had told me about the goings on at Boro, I knew the gates had been closed, I was eight years old, the year previous I was a ballboy for Boro reserves and we had an end of season party at Ayresome Park. We played five-a-side with some of the first team members. Gary Pallister played on my side, I was in awe of him, he was my idol and my favourite player of the time. At school every time I walked past this poster of him I hoped and prayed that Boro were still going to have a team and most of all that Gary Pallister was to be still with us. My prayers were answered. We went from strength to strength and look at us now. I was the happiest person in the world when Gary Pallister re-signed in 1999, I was 21 years old still as big a kid as I had been in 1986. COME ON BORO

Mark Bray

(Now living in Blackpool, still number one Boro fan)

****

I remember being on holiday having a cool beer in an outside bar in Portugal, but unable to totally relax as the out of date newspapers contained no hope for Boro to start the season. On arrival back in England, the first day of the season I got in the car to hear news that they had survived and were playing the Port Vale match at Hartlepool.

After that relief I went to the next match away to Wigan, main memories being their tatty Heinz Stand and the fact that we (around 500 of us) were stood on an open terrace behind the goal covered in grass, no health and safety in those days.

Anyway, Wigan were much the better side but our young kids battled away to half-time. The Wigan fans were mocking of our situation and team and clearly expected to thrash us in the second half. However the Boro grew in confidence and we incredibly won 2-0 and deservedly so because of the determination and team spirit which was to be continued for the rest of that season. Ripley tearing down the wing, Pally and Mowbray rock solid at the back, Pears awesome in goal, Cooper, Parkinson and of course Bernie knocking in the goals as good as any striker you have ever seen.

That season was probably the most enjoyable ever; great away matches at wonderful places like Blackpool, local lads playing their hearts out and we all loved it. The promotion winning game at home to Wigan may have been 0-0 but it was fantastic, everyone on the pitch, the players in the stand throwing out shirts. We didn't want the season to end and tickets for the last match at Doncaster were like gold dust. I remember going down to their ground to try and buy tickets, and queued up at their Portakabin of a ticket office with 100s of other Boro fans.

I was working in Wakefield and the local press advised Doncaster fans that they were unlikely to have much support at the game and that they could refund their tickets! The result was a carnival winning end to the season at Doncaster, in front of a totally Boro crowd, marvellous.

My final memory was the victory celebrations at the town hall, fans climbing up the town hall walls, and hundreds lined up on the roof of the Cleveland Centre draping Boro flags.

A season of loads of terrific memories and Brucie's Boys were to continue on in the same vein for the next few years.

Until then being a Boro fan was an enforced life of misery. I hope the 'new fans' of recent years realise how lucky they are supporting such a fantastic team that wins trophies and regularly gets to cup finals.

In August 1986 you could never have dreamed of the six cup finals (don't forget the Zenith Data, it was amazing at the time), numerous semi-finals and the adventures in Europe.

Glen Minford, Collingham, Wetherby

****

I was 13 years-old when we were in the old third division so I went the matches with my older brother David or my late Uncle Ronnie. I missed only a handful of games that season home and away. On a visit to Wigan early on that season we played some good football and Lee Turnbull scored I think one goal, we won 2-0. I just remember feeling so proud as for three seasons of going away to watch the Boro we had hardly won and to win with such a young team full of local lads against a side that was supposed to be there at the top of the table what a great result. The results started going for us and we were up there at the top all season. In my opinion it was the best season I have ever seen as a Boro fan and many happy journeys home from away games as we were top of the table.

Steven Cook, Redcar
BRUCEY RIOCH's RED & WHITE ARMY

****

The game at the Victoria Ground is my first memory of the Boro. I was eight years old, and my dad took me to watch the game. Although it's all a bit vague now, I remember him lifting me up in the air when we scored and the feeling of excitement as the ball flew in the net. It was a feeling that has since addicted me to the Boro. Now, when I look back knowing the significance of that day, it makes me proud to be able to say that I was there, and look forward to the day when I can tell my children about it. I only hope that their first game can be as significant and unforgettable as my first game, and that they are as grateful to me for taking them as I am to my dad for taking me that fateful day so long ago. It was a day I'll never forget.

David Brownlee

****

I went to the game with Graeme Todd as we always did at Ayresome Park. We started well but faded late on. I remember saying to Graeme, 'If Port Vale are good enough to finish mid-table we can go up' and that's what happened. My greatest memory of the day was the long-range effort by Archie which the cameras only seemed to catch the end of.

R Wilson

****

I can honestly say I was there at Hartlepool 20 years ago with my mate Martyn (Sheffield Wednesday supporter), proof being a photo inside the Bury programme! The memories of that game are of the Boro running out of the Portakabins, Archie Stephens scoring twice, Robbie Earle ruining the party with an equaliser and then the relief of the final whistle as we had gained our first point, which a few weeks earlier never looked as though we would survive the turmoil. Anyway that was the start of an unbelievable journey that brings us to where we are today and without the commitment of Brucie Rioch and the team we would not be in the position we are today. True legends we all remember.

The Riverside Moose, Stockton-on-Tees

****

A wonderful time 1986. A period when so much happened for me and for my team. The personal highlight came the morning after a dreary 0-0 draw at Oakwell, home of Barnsley FC. There, on the doormat, was a letter addressed to me from a promotional company acting on behalf of Shoot football magazine. Inside was notification that I had won the magazine's Football Fan of the Year 1986. The competition started for me with a nomination submitted on my behalf by friend Derek Ferguson. This comprised a report on my support for The Boro, how I stuck by them through thick and thin, through the highs (not all that many at the time) and the lows (plenty of them), how I went to every game home and away, sold lottery tickets for them and all that. There were 16 'Fans of the Week' and I had my turn with that and from the 16 a distinguished panel of football celebrities selected the Fan of the Year. So there I was with a grand presentation down at the Café Royal in London. Frank Bough was the compere with Emlyn Hughes, Trevor Brooking and Mike Flanagan taking part. I don't know whether supporting a team that was having an absolute torrid time of it helped, Frank Bough asked why I supported a team like Middlesbrough that never won anything as he handed me the trophy, 'well at least we've won this' I replied.

The previous season had started with a league game down at Wimbledon to see debuts for Gary Pallister, Gary Rowell and Don O'Riordon, and a one and only appearance for Steve Corden who had the greatest of misfortunes to break a leg in the game and then never make it back to the Boro first team. Boro did nothing in the cups, Mansfield Town got the better of us over two league Cup legs and Southampton beat us 3-1 at Ayresome Park in the FA Cup. One particularly tricky away game was down at Millwall, to help combat crowd trouble Millwall FC decided an answer would be to ban away fans. This was overcome for me by a gratefully received gesture made by Boro chairman Alf Duffield who, hearing of this and my success in the Shoot competition gave up his visiting director's seat at the match for my use. Mr Duffield's esteem rose to greater heights when after the Fan of the Year result was announced he granted me a complimentary season ticket for 1986/87.

It then came as a major disappointment when it was announced as part of the liquidation he was to stand down and no longer have an involvement with the affairs of Middlesbrough Football Club. At the start of that next campaign I did show my award letter from Alf Duffield when applying for a season ticket and guess what, Yes, the new regime stood by it, that's how you get fans for life! Or in my case keep the ones you've got.

The summer of uncertainty lasted forever, or so it seemed. What was going to happen? How painful is this liquidation going to be? Is it terminal? What does a provisional liquidator do, whose interests does he have at heart? How many players do we have left? Will we need them anyway?

So on it went. Daftest question was, 'Who will you support next if Boro fold?'. Not very smart to ask anyone their intentions when a loved one may have a terminal illness, but it was asked.

The release of the fixture list brought home the reality of relegation, first off it's Port Vale of all teams. Boro's competing at the same level as Port blooming Vale! August 23 1986 was a sunny day, there again the opening day of the season always is. In our hour of need Hartlepool FC fished us out in letting us play at the Victoria Ground. So where's the Pool that day? Yes they are at home as well and I decide to go and watch both games, maybe it's the one and only time a ground has hosted two Football League games on the same day. Despite the difficulties of the summer the Boro take the field with only one debutant in young Gary Parkinson who goes on to hold the Boro record for consecutive appearances from debut for a player so far untried anywhere. This was the second time Boro found themselves playing third level football, it was over twenty years ago and twenty years before that Boro were relegated in World Cup year 1966. Both trips had the same duration of a single season with an uplifting finale

Nigel Gibb, Boro fan, Boro statistician.

****

MIDDLESBROUGH ARE SAVED. That headline on the Ceefax football page the Friday night before we were due to play Port Vale brought a huge sigh of relief from myself and I guess a few thousand other Boro supporters. It's only in later years that how close we were to going out of business has been made public, for our nerves that's probably just as well!! Like most Boro fans at the time we'd heard rumours that the club was in debt, so it came as no real surprise when I heard on the radio that the club had been wound up. At the time I wasn't worried, Wolves had done the same, reformed and that was that. However I remember reading in the Gazette the Football League wouldn't allow any other club to do this. What a surprise, we'd be the first team to suffer from this ruling! Anyway the summer for me was spent reading any piece of news regarding people trying to save the club, being gutted when Middlesbrough Council put some money into trying to save the club, only to then have to remove it. I visited Yorkshire Bank added my money to the Save Boro fund and kept my fingers crossed. When I came in from work that Friday afternoon, switched Ceefax on and saw the headline, the relief was tempered by the thought... "How am I getting to Hartlepool tomorrow night?!!!"

Dave Thomas, Boro lad now living in Jarrow.

****

17. Match Facts

IN total 20 players represented Middlesbrough in the 1986-87 season.

Up to November just 13 were used. Paul Proudlock was the first signing after liquidation, though no fee was paid to Hartlepool United for a striker who made just four appearances, was an unused substitute once, and scored four goals. Paul was transferred in March 1989 to Carlisle United where he became something of a hero.

Joining at the same time as Proudlock was Scot Ronnie Coyle, on loan from Glasgow Celtic. He went back to Parkhead, only to return to Ayresome, this time permanently, in March 1987. A defender by trade, Coyle started just two games, was a used sub in four and an unused sub in five. He didn't score. He was released on a free transfer to Rochdale in the August of '87, moving from Spotland to play for Raith Rovers, Ayr United, Albion Rovers, East Fife and Queens Park.

Dave Hodgson had come through Boro's junior ranks to make his debut in 1978. He had stayed for four years before joining Liverpool in 1982. But it was from Norwich City that Boro took him on loan in March 1987. It didn't work out for the winger on his return. He was sent off on his debut away to Bournemouth, going on to start just two more games.

Steve Spriggs is the record appearance holder for Cambridge United. He was signed on loan from the Us in March 1987. The diminutive Doncaster-born defender made just three appearances for Boro – no goals - before leaving in April after refusing a contract.

Gary Rowell made just one non-scoring appearance before joining Brighton in August 1986, while goalkeeper Peter Flear faced the impossible task of dislodging Stephen Pears and made just one non-playing substitute 'appearance' throughout the season.

The only player Boro paid money for in the season of 1986-87 was Paul Kerr. A sum of £50,000 was paid to Aston Villa for the services of the Portsmouth-born midfielder in January 1987. He went on to make 24 appearances and was twice an unused sub. His first of 18 goals for the club didn't come until the sixth game of the following season – ironically against Villa. Paul went on to play for Millwall, Port Vale, Leicester City and Wycombe Wanderers.

Highlights:
Five players played in all 58 games. Stephen Pears, Colin Cooper, Tony Mowbray, Gary Parkinson and Bernie Slaven – all bar Slaven played every minute.

Top scorer was Bernie Slaven with 21; 17 in the league. Next was Archie Stephens with 18; 17 in the league.

Stephen Pears kept 32 clean sheets, 27 in the league.

The average home attendance in the league was 10,174

Match facts from season 1986-87:

Division Three:

Match One
August 23 1986 Victoria Ground, Hartlepool
Middlesbrough 2 Port Vale 2
Goalscorer: Stephens 11, 37
Attendance: 3,690

Pears, Laws, Cooper, Mowbray, Gill, Parkinson, Slaven, Stephens, Hamilton, Kernaghan (Turnbull 87), Ripley.

Match Two
August 30 1986 Springfield Park
Wigan Athletic 0 Middlesbrough 2
Goalscorers: Turnbull 67, Mowbray 75
Attendance: 2,904

Pears, Laws, Cooper, Mowbray, Parkinson, Pallister, Slaven, Turnbull, Hamilton, Gill, Ripley. Unused sub. Kernaghan.

Match Three
September 6 1986 Ayresome Park
Middlesbrough 3 Bury 1
Goalscorers: Stephens 4, 58, Slaven 67
Attendance: 6,499

Pears, Laws, Cooper, Mowbray, Parkinson, Pallister, Slaven, Stephens, Hamilton, Gill, Ripley. Unused sub. Turnbull.

Match Four
September 13 1986 Priestfield Stadium
Gillingham 0 Middlesbrough 0
Attendance: 4,888

Pears, Laws, Cooper, Mowbray, Parkinson, Pallister, Slaven, Stephens, Hamilton, Gill, Ripley. Unused sub. Turnbull.

Match Five
September 17 1986 Eastville
Bristol Rovers 1 Middlesbrough 2
Goalscorer: Slaven 33, 68
Attendance: 3,768

Pears, Laws, Cooper, Mowbray, Parkinson, Pallister, Slaven, Stephens, Hamilton, Gill, Ripley. Unused sub. Turnbull.

Match Six
September 20 1986 Ayresome Park
Middlesbrough 2 Chesterfield 0
Goalscorers: Mowbray 65, Laws 71
Attendance: 7,633

Pears, Laws, Cooper, Mowbray, Parkinson, Pallister, Slaven (Turnbull 90), Stephens, Hamilton, Gill, Ripley.

Match Seven
September 27 1986 Craven Cottage
Fulham 2 Middlesbrough 2
Goalscorers: Laws 14, Hamilton 24
Attendance: 3,852

Pears, Laws, Cooper, Mowbray, Parkinson, Pallister, Slaven, Stephens, Hamilton, Gill, Ripley. Unused sub. Turnbull.

Match Eight
September 30 1986 Ayresome Park
Middlesbrough 1 Swindon Town 0
Goalscorer: Laws 36
Attendance: 9,221

Pears, Laws, Cooper, Mowbray, Parkinson, Pallister, Slaven, Stephens, Hamilton, Gill, Ripley. Unused sub. Turnbull.

Match Nine
October 4 1986 Millmoor
Rotherham United 1 Middlesbrough 4
Goalscorers: Stephens 8, 18, Laws 55, 83
Attendance: 4,321

Pears, Laws, Cooper, Mowbray, Parkinson, Pallister, Slaven, Stephens, Hamilton, Gill, Ripley. Unused sub. Kernaghan.

Match Ten
October 11 1986 Ayresome Park
Middlesbrough 1 Blackpool 3
Goalscorer: Stephens 76
Attendance: 11,470

Pears, Laws, Cooper, Mowbray, Parkinson, Pallister, Slaven (Kernaghan 56), Stephens, Hamilton, Gill, Ripley.

Match Eleven
October 18 1986 Ayresome Park
Middlesbrough 3 Walsall 1
Goalscorers: Stephens 2, 68, Laws 15
Attendance: 8,349

Pears, Laws, Cooper, Mowbray, Parkinson, Pallister, Slaven, Stephens, Hamilton, Gill, Ripley. Unused sub. Turnbull.

Match Twelve
October 21 1986 Meadow Lane
Notts County 1 Middlesbrough 0
Attendance: 4,405

Pears, Laws, Cooper, Mowbray, Parkinson, Pallister, Slaven, Stephens, Hamilton, Gill, Ripley (Turnbull 83).

Match Thirteen
October 25 1986 Ashton Gate
Bristol City 2 Middlesbrough 2
Goalscorers: Slaven 24, Laws 35
Attendance: 8,800

Pears, Laws, Cooper, Mowbray, Parkinson, Pallister, Slaven, Stephens, Hamilton, Gill, Ripley. Unused sub. Turnbull.

Match Fourteen
November 1 1986 Ayresome Park
Middlesbrough 4 Bournemouth 0
Goalscorers: Stephens 23, Slaven 43, Hamilton 57, Ripley 72
Attendance: 10,702

Pears, Laws, Cooper, Mowbray, Parkinson, Pallister, Slaven, Stephens, Hamilton, Gill (Turnbull 87), Ripley.

Match Fifteen
November 4 1986 Ayresome Park
Middlesbrough 0 Bolton Wanderers 0
Attendance: 10,092

Pears, Laws, Cooper, Mowbray, Parkinson, Pallister, Slaven, Stephens, Hamilton (Turnbull 74), Gill, Ripley.

Match Sixteen
November 8 1986 Feethams
Darlington 0 Middlesbrough 1
Goalscorer: Stephens 64
Attendance: 9,947

Pears, Laws, Cooper, Mowbray, Parkinson, Pallister, Slaven, Stephens, Kernaghan, Gill, Ripley. Unused sub: Turnbull.

Match Seventeen
November 22 1986 Somerton Park
Newport County 0 Middlesbrough 1
Goalscorer: Mowbray 89
Attendance: 2,788

Pears, Laws, Cooper, Mowbray, Parkinson, Pallister, Slaven, Stephens, Kernaghan (Hamilton 72), Gill, Ripley.

Match Eighteen
November 29 1986 Ayresome Park
Middlesbrough 1 Chester City 2
Goalscorer: Slaven 16
Attendance: 9,376

Pears, Laws, Cooper, Mowbray, Parkinson, Pallister, Slaven, Stephens, Kernaghan, Gill (Hamilton 66), Ripley.

Match Nineteen
December 13 1986 Ayresome Park
Middlesbrough 1 Doncaster Rovers 0
Goalscorer: Mowbray 31
Attendance: 8,100

Pears, Laws, Cooper, Mowbray, Parkinson, Pallister, Slaven, Stephens, Hamilton, Gill, Proudlock. Unused sub: Coyle.

Match Twenty
December 21 1986 Griffin Park
Brentford 0 Middlesbrough 1
Goalscorer: Slaven 17
Attendance: 5,504

Pears, Laws, Cooper, Mowbray, Parkinson, Pallister, Slaven, Stephens (Proudlock 85), Hamilton, Gill, Ripley.

Match Twenty One
December 26 1986 Ayresome Park
Middlesbrough 1 Carlisle United 0
Goalscorer: Gill 67
Attendance: 14,216

Pears, Laws, Cooper, Mowbray, Parkinson, Pallister, Slaven, Stephens, Hamilton, Gill, Ripley. Unused sub: Proudlock.

Match Twenty Two
December 27 1986 Field Mill
Mansfield Town 1 Middlesbrough 1
Goalscorer: Proudlock 71
Attendance: 5,042

Pears, Laws, Cooper, Mowbray, Parkinson, Pallister, Slaven, Proudlock (Coyle 83), Hamilton, Gill, Ripley.

Match Twenty Three
January 1 1987 Bootham Crescent
York City 3 Middlesbrough 1
Goalscorer: Mowbray 46
Attendance: 8,611

Pears, Laws, Cooper, Mowbray, Parkinson, Pallister, Slaven, Stephens, Hamilton, Gill, Ripley. Unused sub: Kernaghan.

Match Twenty Four
January 3 1987 Ayresome Park
Middlesbrough 2 Newport County 0
Goalscorers: Gill 46, Stephens 75
Attendance: 9,595

Pears, Laws, Cooper, Mowbray, Parkinson, Pallister, Slaven, Stephens, Hamilton, Gill, Ripley. Unused sub: Coyle.

Match Twenty Five
January 24 1987 Gigg Lane
Bury 0 Middlesbrough 3
Goalscorers: Slaven 13, 89, Laws 36 (pen)
Attendance: 3,385

Pears, Laws, Cooper, Mowbray, Parkinson, Pallister, Slaven, Stephens, Kerr, Gill, Ripley. Unused sub: Kernaghan.

Match Twenty Six
February 7 1987 Ayresome Park
Middlesbrough 1 Bristol Rovers 0
Goalscorer: Ripley 60
Attendance: 9,610

Pears, Laws (Kernaghan 46), Cooper, Mowbray, Parkinson, Pallister, Slaven, Stephens, Kerr, Gill, Ripley.

Match Twenty Seven
February 14 1987 Saltergate
Chesterfield 2 Middlesbrough 1
Goalscorer: Slaven 4
Attendance: 4,085

Pears, Hamilton, Cooper, Mowbray, Parkinson, Pallister, Slaven, Stephens, Kerr, Gill, Ripley. Unused sub: Kernaghan.

Match Twenty Eight
February 17 1987 Vale Park
Port Vale 0 Middlesbrough 0
Attendance: 3,263

Pears, Hamilton, Cooper, Mowbray, Parkinson, Pallister, Slaven, Stephens, Kerr, Gill, Ripley. Unused sub: Kernaghan.

Match Twenty Nine
February 21 1987 Ayresome Park
Middlesbrough 3 Fulham 0
Goalscorers: Slaven 9, Hamilton 54,71
Attendance: 9,361

Pears, Hamilton, Cooper, Mowbray, Parkinson, Pallister, Slaven, Stephens, Kerr, Gill, Ripley. Unused sub: Kernaghan.

Match Thirty
February 28 1987 County Ground
Swindon Town 1 Middlesbrough 0
Attendance: 11,341

Pears, Hamilton, Cooper, Mowbray, Parkinson, Pallister, Slaven, Stephens, Kerr, Kernaghan, Ripley. Unused sub: Turnbull.

Match Thirty One
March 3 1987 Dean Court
Bournemouth 3 Middlesbrough 1
Goalscorer: Slaven 53
Attendance: 13,835

Pears, Hamilton, Cooper, Mowbray, Parkinson, Pallister (Ripley 42), Slaven, Stephens, Kerr, Kernaghan, Hodgson.

Match Thirty Two
March 7 1987 Ayresome Park
Middlesbrough 1 Bristol City 0
Goalscorer: Mowbray 36
Attendance: 10,220

Pears, Coyle, Cooper, Mowbray, Parkinson, Kernaghan, Slaven, Stephens, Hamilton, Gill, Hodgson. Unused sub: Kerr.

Match Thirty Three
March 14 1987 Fellows Park
Walsall 1 Middlesbrough 0
Attendance: 7,332

Pears, Hamilton, Cooper, Mowbray, Parkinson, Pallister, Slaven, Stephens (Kernaghan 72), Kerr, Gill, Ripley.

Match Thirty Four
March 17 1987 Ayresome Park
Middlesbrough 2 Notts County 0
Goalscorers: Stephens 65, Slaven 87
Attendance: 9,845

Pears, Kernaghan, Cooper, Mowbray, Parkinson, Pallister, Slaven, Stephens, Kerr, Hamilton, Ripley. Unused sub: Coyle.

Match Thirty Five
March 21 1987 Bloomfield Road
Blackpool 0 Middlesbrough 1
Goalscorer: Stephens 53
Attendance: 7,132

Pears, Kernaghan (Gill 78), Cooper, Mowbray, Parkinson, Pallister, Slaven, Stephens, Kerr, Hamilton, Ripley.

Match Thirty Six
March 28 1987 Ayresome Park
Middlesbrough 0 Rotherham United 0
Attendance: 9,569

Pears, Kernaghan (Gill 69), Cooper, Mowbray, Parkinson, Pallister, Slaven, Stephens, Kerr, Hamilton, Ripley.

Match Thirty Seven
April 5 1987 Ayresome Park
Middlesbrough 1 Darlington 1
Goalscorer: Slaven 66
Attendance: 11,969

Pears, Spriggs, Cooper, Mowbray, Parkinson, Pallister, Slaven, Stephens, Hamilton, Gill, Ripley. Unused sub: Kerr.

Match Thirty Eight
April 11 1987 Burnden Park
Bolton Wanderers 0 Middlesbrough 1
Goalscorer: Slaven 87
Attendance: 5,858

Pears, Spriggs, Cooper, Mowbray, Parkinson, Pallister, Slaven, Stephens, Hamilton, Kerr, Ripley. Unused sub: Gill.

Match Thirty Nine
April 18 1987 Ayresome Park
Middlesbrough 3 York City 1
Goalscorers: Ripley 40, Stephens 71, Turnbull 88
Attendance: 10,546

Pears, Spriggs (Turnbull 18), Cooper, Mowbray, Parkinson, Pallister, Slaven, Stephens, Hamilton, Kerr, Ripley.

Match Forty
April 20 1987 Brunton Park
Carlisle United 0 Middlesbrough 1
Goalscorer: Pallister 19
Attendance: 5,993

Pears, Hamilton, Cooper, Mowbray, Parkinson, Pallister, Slaven, Stephens, Turnbull, Kerr, Ripley. Unused sub: Coyle.

Match Forty One
April 25 1987 Ayresome Park
Middlesbrough 2 Brentford 0
Goalscorers: Slaven 2, Turnbull 44
Attendance: 9,942

Pears, Hamilton, Cooper, Mowbray, Parkinson, Pallister, Slaven, Stephens, Turnbull, Kerr, Ripley. Unused sub: Coyle.

Match Forty Two
April 28 1987 Ayresome Park
Middlesbrough 3 Gillingham 0
Goalscorers: Stephens 3, Slaven 10, Turnbull 47
Attendance: 11,937

Pears, Hamilton, Cooper, Mowbray, Parkinson, Pallister, Slaven (Coyle 88), Stephens, Turnbull, Kerr, Ripley.

Match Forty Three

May 2 1987 Sealand Road
Chester City 1 Middlesbrough 2
Goalscorers: Mowbray 29, Hamilton 66
Attendance: 3,788

Pears, Hamilton, Cooper, Mowbray, Parkinson, Pallister, Slaven, Stephens, Turnbull, Kerr, Ripley. Unused sub: Gill.

Match Forty Four

May 4 1987 Ayresome Park
Middlesbrough 1 Mansfield Town 0
Goalscorer: Hamilton 58 (pen)
Attendance: 13,545

Pears, Hamilton, Cooper, Mowbray, Parkinson, Pallister, Slaven, Stephens, Turnbull (Gill 86), Kerr, Ripley.

Match Forty Five

May 6 1987 Ayresome Park
Middlesbrough 0 Wigan Athletic 0
Attendance: 18,523

Pears, Hamilton, Cooper, Mowbray, Parkinson, Pallister, Slaven, Stephens, Turnbull, Kerr, Ripley. Unused sub: Gill.

Match Forty Six

May 9 1987 Belle Vue
Doncaster Rovers 0 Middlesbrough 2
Goalscorers: Hamilton 26, Ripley 60
Attendance: 3,556

Pears, Gill, Cooper, Mowbray, Parkinson, Pallister, Slaven, Stephens, Hamilton (Turnbull 76), Kerr, Ripley.

League Cup:

Round One First Leg
August 26 1986 Victoria Ground
Hartlepool United 1 Middlesbrough 1
Goalscorer: Slaven 57
Attendance: 2,356

Pears, Laws, Cooper, Mowbray, Parkinson, Gill, Slaven, Stephens, Hamilton, Rowell (Kernaghan 74), Ripley. Unused sub: Turnbull.

Round One Second Leg
September 2 1986 Ayresome Park
Middlesbrough 2 Hartlepool United 0
Goalscorers: Ripley 31, Hamilton 85
Attendance: 7,735

Pears, Laws, Cooper, Mowbray, Parkinson, Pallister, Slaven, Stephens (Turnbull 28), Hamilton, Gill, Ripley. Unused sub: Kernaghan.

Round Two First Leg
September 23 1986 Ayresome Park
Middlesbrough 2 Birmingham City 2
Goalscorers: Stephens 10, Ripley 89
Attendance: 9,412

Pears, Laws, Cooper, Mowbray, Parkinson, Pallister, Slaven, Stephens, Hamilton, Gill, Ripley. Unused subs: Kernaghan, Turnbull.

Round Two Second Leg
October 7 1986 St Andrews
Birmingham City 3 Middlesbrough 2 (After extra time)
Goalscorer: Laws 1, 117 (Pen)
Attendance: 4,978

Pears, Laws, Cooper, Mowbray, Parkinson, Pallister, Slaven, Stephens, Hamilton, Gill (Kernaghan 110), Ripley. Unused sub: Turnbull.

FA Cup

Round One
November 15 1986 Ayresome Park
Middlesbrough 3 Blackpool 0
Goalscorer: Slaven 18, 70, 76
Attendance: 11,205

Pears, Laws, Cooper, Mowbray, Parkinson, Pallister, Slaven, Stephens, Kernaghan, Gill, Ripley. Unused subs: Flear (gk), Hamilton

---

Round Two
December 7 1986 Meadow Lane
Notts County 0 Middlesbrough 1
Goalscorer: Hamilton 54
Attendance: 7,415

Pears, Laws, Cooper, Mowbray, Parkinson, Pallister, Slaven, Stephens, Hamilton, Gill, Ripley. Unused subs: Kernaghan, Turnbull

---

Round Three
January 10 1987 Ayresome Park
Middlesbrough 0 Preston North End 1
Attendance: 15,458

Pears, Laws (Kernaghan 50), Cooper, Mowbray, Parkinson, Pallister, Slaven, Kerr (Coyle 50), Hamilton, Gill, Ripley.

Freight Rover Trophy

Preliminary Round
November 24 1986 Ayresome Park
Middlesbrough 3 Doncaster Rovers 0
Goalscorers: Proudlock 7, 80, Turnbull 86
Attendance: 3,977

Pears, Laws, Cooper, Mowbray, Parkinson, Pallister, Slaven (Turnbull 83), Proudlock, Hamilton (Kernaghan 87), Gill, Ripley.

Preliminary Round
December 2 1986 Saltergate
Chesterfield 2 Middlesbrough 1
Goalscorer: Stephens 42
Attendance: 1,764

Pears, Laws, Cooper, Mowbray, Parkinson, Pallister, Slaven, Stephens, Hamilton, Gill, Ripley. Unused subs: Kernaghan, Proudlock

---

Round One
January 21 1987 The Shay
Halifax Town 1 Middlesbrough 2
Goalscorers: Kernaghan 29, Ripley 87
Attendance: 1,411

Pears, Kernaghan, Cooper, Mowbray, Parkinson, Pallister, Slaven, Kerr, Hamilton, Gill, Ripley. No subs.

Round Two
February 10 1987 Spotland
Rochdale 0 Middlesbrough 0 (Boro won 4-3 on penalties: Stephens, Cooper, Slaven, Hamilton)
Attendance: 2,615

Pears, Kernaghan (Coyle 105), Cooper, Mowbray, Parkinson, Pallister, Slaven, Stephens, Kerr, Gill, Ripley (Hamilton 105).

Area Semi Final
March 10 1987 Ayresome Park
Middlesbrough 0 Mansfield Town 1
Attendance: 11,754

Pears, Coyle (Kerr 79), Cooper, Mowbray, Parkinson, Kernaghan, Slaven, Stephens, Hamilton, Gill, Hodgson (Ripley 70).

Date		Oppostion	Home/Away	Res.	Scorers	Att.
Aug	23	Port Vale	H	2-2	Stephens 2	3,690
	30	Wigan A	A	2-0	Turnbull, Mowbray	2,904
Sep	6	Bury	H	3-1	Stephens 2, Slaven	6,499
	13	Gillingham	A	0-0		4,888
	17	Bristol R	A	2-1	Slaven 2	3,768
	20	Chesterfield	H	2-0	Mowbray, Laws	7,633
	27	Fulham	A	2-2	Laws, Hamilton	3,852
	30	Swindon T	H	1-0	Laws	9,221
Oct	4	Rotherham	A	4-1	Stephens 2, Laws 2	4,321
	11	Blackpool	H	1-3	Stephens	11,470
	18	Walsall	H	3-1	Stephens 2, Laws	8,349
	21	Notts Co	A	0-1		4,405
	25	Bristol C	A	2-2	Slaven, Laws	8,800
Nov	1	Bournemouth	H	4-0	Stephens, Slaven, Hamilton Ripley	10,702
	4	Bolton W	H	0-0		10,092
	8	Darlington	A	1-0	Stephens	9,947
	22	Newport Co	A	1-0	Mowbray	2,788
	29	Chester C	H	1-2	Slaven	9,376
Dec	13	Doncaster R	H	1-0	Mowbray	8,100
	21	Brentford	A	1-0	Slaven	5,504
	26	Carlisle U	H	1-0	Gill	14,216
	27	Mansfield T	A	1-1	Proudlock	5,042
Jan	1	York C	A	1-3	Mowbray	8,611
	3	Newport Co	H	2-0	Gill, Stephens	9,595
	24	Bury	A	3-0	Slaven 2, Laws (pen)	3,485
Feb	7	Bristol R	H	1-0	Ripley	9,610
	14	Chesterfield	A	1-2	Slaven	4,085
	17	Port Vale	A	0-0		3,263
	21	Fulham	H	3-0	Slaven, Hamilton 2	9,361
	28	Swindon T	A	0-1		11,341
Mar	3	Bournemouth	A	1-3	Slaven	13,835
	7	Bristol C	H	1-0	Mowbray	10,220
	14	Walsall	A	0-1		7,332
	17	Notts Co	H	2-0	Stephens, Slaven	9,845
	21	Blackpool	A	1-0	Stephens	7,132
	28	Rotherham	H	0-0		9,569
Apr	5	Darlington	H	1-1	Slaven	11,969
	11	Bolton W	A	1-0	Slaven	5,858
	18	York C	H	3-1	Ripley, Stephens, Turnbull	10,546
	20	Carlisle U	A	1-0	Pallister	5,993
	25	Brentford	H	2-0	Slaven, Turnbull	9,942
	28	Gillingham	H	3-0	Stephens, Slaven. Turnbull	11,937
May	2	Chester C	A	2-1	Mowbray, Hamilton	3,788
	4	Mansfield T	H	1-0	Hamilton (pen)	13,543
	6	Wigan A	H	0-0		18,523
	9	Doncaster R	A	2-0	Hamilton, Ripley	3,556

	P	HW	HD	HL	HGF	HGA	AW	AD	AL	AGF	AGA	Points	GD
Bournemouth	46	19	3	1	44	14	10	7	6	32	26	97	+36
BORO	**46**	**16**	**5**	**2**	**38**	**11**	**12**	**5**	**6**	**29**	**19**	**94**	**+37**
Swindon Town	46	14	5	4	37	19	11	7	5	40	28	87	+30
Wigan	46	15	5	3	47	26	10	5	8	36	34	85	+23
Gillingham	46	16	5	2	42	14	7	4	12	23	34	78	+17
Bristol City	46	14	6	3	42	15	7	8	8	21	21	77	+27
Notts County	46	14	6	3	52	24	7	7	9	25	32	76	+21
Walsall	46	16	4	3	50	27	6	5	12	30	40	75	+13
Blackpool	46	11	7	5	35	20	5	9	9	39	39	64	+15
Mansfield Town	46	9	9	5	30	23	6	7	10	22	32	61	-3
Brentford	46	9	7	7	39	32	6	8	9	25	34	60	-2
Port Vale	46	8	6	9	43	36	7	6	10	33	34	57	+6
Doncaster	46	11	8	4	32	19	3	7	13	24	43	57	-6
Rotherham	46	10	6	7	29	23	5	6	12	19	34	57	-9
Chester	46	7	9	7	32	28	6	8	9	29	31	56	+2
Bury	46	9	7	7	30	26	5	6	12	24	34	55	-6
Chesterfield	46	11	5	7	36	33	2	10	11	20	36	54	-13
Fulham	46	8	8	7	35	41	4	9	10	24	36	53	-18
Bristol Rovers	46	7	8	8	26	29	6	4	13	23	46	51	-26
York City	46	11	8	4	34	29	1	5	17	21	50	49	-24
Bolton	46	8	5	10	29	26	2	10	11	17	32	45	-12
Carlisle	46	7	5	11	26	35	3	3	17	13	43	38	-39
Darlington	46	6	10	7	25	28	1	6	16	20	49	37	-32
Newport County	46	4	9	10	26	34	4	4	15	23	52	37	-37

THE TODAY LEAGUE DIVISION III

WEDNESDAY 6th MAY, 1987

MIDDLESBROUGH v. WIGAN

KICK OFF 7.30 p.m.

BORO NE
VIEWS & FEATUR

Tonight's Match Sponsors
TANKFREIGHT

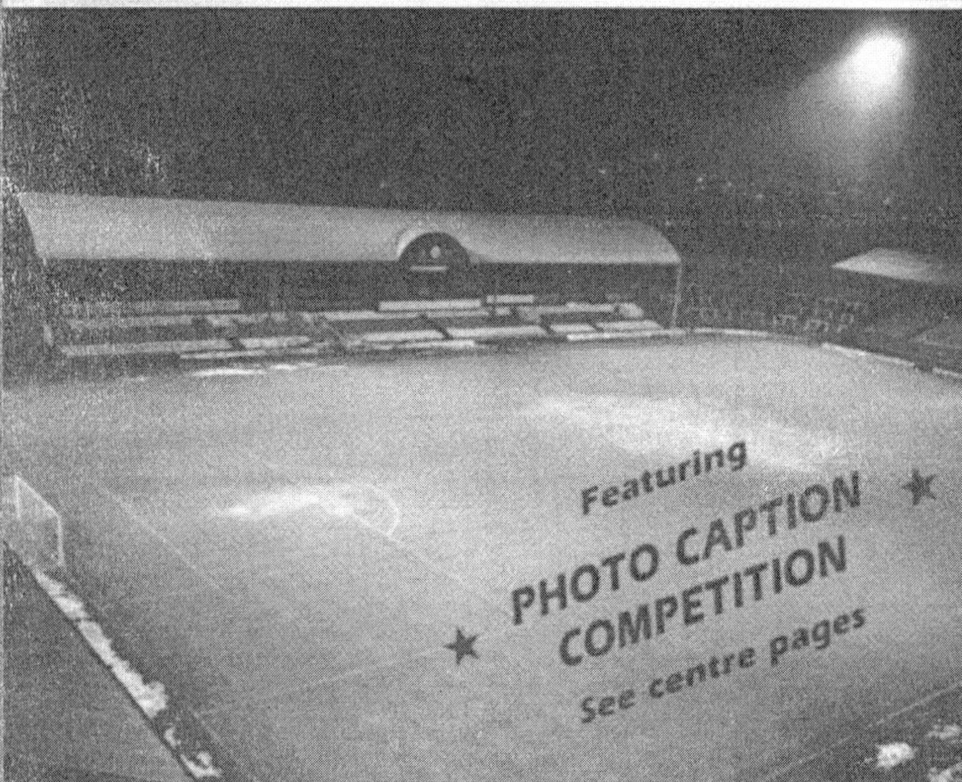

MIDDLESBROUGH

FOOTBALL CLUB

OFFICIAL PROGRAMME

50p

DICKENS

Official Sponsors 1987/8